SEA VIEW

SEA VIEW

A year of reflective glimpses into life in Shetland

Alastair Christie-Johnston

The Shetland Times Ltd.
Lerwick
2011

Sea View

Copyright © Alastair Christie-Johnston, 2011.

Alastair Christie-Johnston has asserted his right under the Copyright, Designs and Patents Act, 1998, to be identified as the author of this work.

ISBN 978-1-904746-61-4

First published by The Shetland Times Ltd., 2011.

A catalogue record for this book is available from the British Library.

All rights reserved.
No part of this publication may be reproduced, stored in a retrieval system, or transmitted, in any form, by any means, electronic, mechanical, photocopying, recording or otherwise, without the prior written permission of the publishers.

Cover photo: Aywick Beach.
(Boat digitally named with kind permission of its owner, Connor Thompson.)

Printed and published by
The Shetland Times Ltd.,
Gremista, Lerwick, Shetland
ZE1 0PX, Scotland.

For
Ethan Magnus

The sea, once it casts its spell, holds one in its net of wonder forever.
Jacques Yves Cousteau

SEA VIEW

BATTLESHIP grey of sky and sea are welded together in an indistinguishable graft. Nearer at hand gulls are riding the gentle swell in which white crescents are raised eyebrows of seemingly endless repetitive query into what the day might bring. I press my nose to the porthole, angling for a nor-easterly vista in which I hope for a first glimpse of Bressay (pronounced Bressa in Shetland). At the eastern extremity of which is the island of Noss, its cliff-face – the Noup – known to birdwatchers from all over Europe, many of whom come during spring and summer to marvel at the myriad seabirds nesting here. But it will be another half hour before any of this will hove into sight. For the time being I must be content with knowing this is the sea of my childhood and I have come home. Tomorrow I will look at it from the perspective of terra firma. I might walk down to the shore and dip my hand into the cold briny. I might skim a stone, pick up a shell, listen to the waves lapping the rocky beach, catch a ferry or row out and drop a line. I might do all manner of salty seafaring things. Today I will be content to know I have arrived.

Day two begins with a westward view across the water from my temporary base in Bressay (60° 09′ N; 1° 07′ W) to the grey crenulations of the old town, Lerwick, which is the hub of Shetland and a five-minute ferry trip away. It is a stark change from the gaily painted weatherboard and red brick houses of my life in Hobart, Tasmania, and even more so from the prefabricated 'baches' of Waiheke Island, New Zealand, where I have spent the last three months. I have switched more than seasons – spring to autumn. The sun's trajectory has changed from north to south and upset my internal compass. The Southern Cross has vanished out of my night-time sky and I must again take my bearings from the Pole Star or the Great Bear. Even the loose change in my pocket is confusing me. And the sea… it is *so* different.

Someone recently tried to reassure me that all the seas of the world are interconnected and the same water that laps the shores of Pacific islands may, in time, carry a message-bottle or piece of driftwood across the world and deliver it to where I am now standing. Why, then, does this sea appear so coldly uninviting when the one I left languidly caressing white sands in New Zealand is an iridescent aqua that looks like the polished surface of pau shell and begs me to dive into its warm embrace and swim out to the sunset? Give me a little time and I will adjust. As jetlag is to air travel so a sea change requires a day or two to tide us over.

Feeling the need to connect with this new environment, I climb the Ward of Bressay (225m). Not what you might term a mountain, but not a molehill either. From the top, the entire coastline of Bressay is visible. Surrounding the island and scarcely ruffled by the breeze, the royally blue sea wears a lace-fringed hap. Air is fresh as newly popped champagne and comes with a heather bouquet. Too much of this and I will become light-headed.

The North Boat (some call it the South Boat) is heading up past the Knab to her berth. A tall ship has sneaked in before dawn, or at least before it has dawned on me. She is the barque *Statsraad Lehmkuhl*, a regular visitor from Norway. Ferried across the harbour mid-morning I drink in the sights and sounds, still needing to pinch myself occasionally to be sure this is all real.

A car drive to the most northerly district of Shetland's mainland includes several detours to take in all the angles. Not being responsible for driving means I can make the most of sightseeing. It also means I become hopelessly disorientated. "Is that Papa Stour over there or...?" "Yes, yes. On a better day you can see Foula."

Five minutes later we are looking across Yell Sound to West Sandwick on the island of Yell and that, by the way, is another sea change – North Atlantic to North Sea.

Every voe we pass seems to be dotted with mussel rafts or salmon cages. I'm told it is a £90 million a year industry. What would the old 'haaf' fishermen have made of it; rowing out beyond sight of land in their six-oared boats and bringing back their modest catches only to forfeit the greater part (if not all) to greedy landlords. Subsistence living now changed to subsidised living thanks to EU policies and the good work of the Crofter's Commission.

Our return to Lerwick includes yet another detour, this time via Voe and Aith. In the intervening thirty years since I last took this route one of the most notable and pleasing changes is the reduction in the amount of litter. The beaches and roadsides used to be festooned with all manner of 'bruck', especially plastic containers and frayed ends of orange and blue nylon rope. It is certainly a change for the better.

Lerwick harbour is buzzing. Peerie sails skittishly dancing around buoys in a sungaets Shetland Reel while the Bressay ferry cuts cross-grained through them – a contrary fishwife in a flower shop.

A few miles west of Lerwick on the Atlantic coast lies the ancient capital of Scalloway. The town's narrow and largely unspoiled winding streets lead down to what is still a busy little fishing port. I could easily fall in love with this place with its lovely old houses, pretty courtyards filled with trees and its stunning sunset views.

Walking to the north end of Bressay – about a seven mile round trip from the house in which my wife Adaline and I are staying – I cross the strand at

SEA VIEW

Minni of Aith to Aith Ness. A rusted First World War six-inch gun sits atop Score Hill where it presumably guarded the northern entrance to Bressay Sound and Lerwick Harbour. Nearby are the concrete foundations of what may have been a barracks or Nissan Hut for those on duty in this lonely spot. Did they ever fire a shot in anger? The gun is pointed at the northernmost extremity of Bressay – Outer Score, Inner Score, Score Head and Score Minni. Is this nomenclature someone's idea of a joke derived from target practice?

Nearby are the remains of a quarry from which stone was used in the construction of many of Lerwick's early buildings, including the Town Hall. Walls in the vicinity (some appear to have been built for no other purpose than to show off the superior quality of the material) are amongst the best examples of dry-stone work I have seen in the islands.

Having arranged temporary rental housing pending council allocation of something more permanent, we set off via two ferry crossings to the north isle of Yell. This relatively remote island will be our home for the next six months. Incidentally, it is the island of our birth and, in Adaline's case, where she has lived for the greater part of her life. The village we move to is called Mid Yell which (not surprisingly) is situated in the centre of the island. The outlook from the house gives one the impression of what it might be like to live in a fish bowl, with the voe (and presumably fish) at the bottom, surrounded by houses lining the upper sides and rim. We are on the south-eastern part of the rim and directly above the pier where daily activity provides a source of regular distraction. *Conquest*, a snub-nosed custom-built vessel, plies to and from nearby salmon cages bringing her 'catch' to be pumped into waiting containers that are hauled off by lorries to who-knows-where for factory processing. To the untrained eye it all appears to be very straightforward and uncomplicated. Perhaps when winter gales set in it will be a different kettle of fish.

Now, with suitcases unpacked and our few possessions sorted, I set out to walk southward over the hill of Lussetter to Vatsetter. Sphagnum moss is almost knee deep in places and with a blustery headwind I make heavy going of it. Vatsetter loch looks a promising prospect for trout. Too bad the season ends in a couple of weeks. *Conquest* is in attendance alongside salmon cages in the lee of Hascosay, the island that guards Mid Yell voe. If this is all the distance they go to harvest the sea it would appear *Conquest* is something of an exaggeration.

The strip of sand on the shore below the house has two plastic fish boxes buried in it up to their rims. One is yellow and one is blue. I could dig them out as a gesture towards environmental tidiness or I could leave them for the sea to complete its undertaking to bury them completely. Man has wrought countless ecological disasters on seas and seashores around the world yet in virtually every case the all-forgiving ocean has wiped away every trace and repaired the damage. This by no means exonerates us from our follies but it does seem that Neptune is a remarkably tolerant fellow.

I recall reading Lillian Beckwith's engaging novels about life in the Western Isles. One of her first books was called *The Sea for Breakfast*. And now, all these years later, I am at last discovering the hidden nuances in that title. Waking to sights and sounds of the sea, enjoying 'catch of the day' (with the catcher occasionally sharing my table) and, by the way, haddock caught hereabouts are simply the best in the world; the sea for breakfast has become an actual experience rather than merely a good read. I love its fickle ways, its stormy scenes giving out to soothing swells. Rocking the boat one minute, becalming it the next. Turbulent to torpid on a whimsical wind shift.

There are footprints in the sand leading to two holes where the fish boxes used to be. It seems this jetsam has some value. A man is at the ebb washing the rewards of his beachcombing. An open-backed van at the side of the road awaits his catch. Within six hours sea will have obliterated all trace of this activity.

Little wonder it sighs so much when it is always left to clean up man's mess.

Flashback

The flight over central Australia is at 30,000ft on a cloudless night of full moon. With a window seat towards the back of the plane I have a good view and am amazed at the clarity of the scene. The ridged desert is a rolling sea with dark rocky outcrops appearing as islands. Later, over the archipelago of Indonesia, every bay is spangled with stars. They are the night fishermen. Hundreds of them, each hoping to land a prize catch and be first at the dawn market. Cocooned as I am in this miracle of modern technology speeding across the world, it is difficult to imagine what it must have been like a hundred and fifty years ago when distant travel inevitably meant a sea voyage under sail. What this plane will accomplish in a few hours required months of deprivation and danger. About the only similarity is the cramped quarters and I need endure this for less than a day, with every kind of diversionary entertainment to take my mind off it. Then again, a canting deck in a flying gale is a sight closer to our primeval roots than this travelling on the edge of space. In the beginning we all came out of the sea and many of us still feel more at home when we are closest to it.

With a fresh northerly wind, broken cloud and intermittent sunshine we drive north to Cullivoe and Breckon. On such days the Blue Mull (the cliff facing Cullivoe) has a magic all its own. The side road north out of Gutcher is signed 'Cullivoe' and 'The Gloup Memorial'. Tourists tend to hurry past on their way to catch the ferry for Unst, eager to reach Hermaness and the bird rookeries there. Few guess at the scenic beauty that surrounds Cullivoe, Breckon and Gloup – especially Breckon where the beach is one of Shetland's finest *(see photo page ii)*. Okay, I admit to a certain bias but Cullivoe is my birthplace, my 'bonhoga', and so you will have to permit the rose-tinted glasses.

Wind has veered to the north-west and become colder. When the sun shines, the sea is aquamarine turning to pewter whenever cloud slides its shutter across. Sky is duck-egg at the horizon. For the first day since we arrived here all the boats have left the pier. Bundles of nets have gone too. In the exposed reaches west of Unst, up towards Muckle Flugga, seas will be rough. I wonder where the fishing fleet has gone. Not far, it seems, for they come and go through the voe as the day wears on, muscling out from behind Gardiestang beyond which lies the marina at the head of the voe; chugging back hours later, stern down with who-knows-what in their holds.

During the night the wind drops, bringing a 'platt maalie caalm' morning, as they say in North Yell. It is not difficult to interpret the meaning of the words though their origin is somewhat obscure. Flat calm – mirror calm, if you will. Driving to Lerwick the lochs reflect the surrounding moorland so perfectly I have difficulty keeping my eyes on the road. The low trajectory of the sun at this time of year affords exquisite light effects in the folds of the hills, picking out details with the precision of a cameo carver. The moor has more furrows than an old man's brow.

After heavy rain all the burns and ditches are running in spate. Forecast weather and associated cancellation of ferries has not materialised, in fact we appear to be in the eye of the storm. An uneasy calm. Doubtless the change will come and so I decide to go for a hike while I have the chance. A short drive to North-a-Voe and I set out for the coast overlooking Hascosay. Crossing the Burn of Kaywick, I pass a ruined house (Kaywick) overlooking Kay Holm at the entrance to Mid Yell Voe. (Who or what was 'Kay' to deserve so much nomenclature?) Further out, perhaps half a mile offshore, lies the island of Hascosay, shaped like a fat fish-hook. Fetlar lies beyond. The juxtaposition of these various islands creates hazardous or enjoyable sailing depending on the weather. At the moment it is calm, making the outlook peaceful and pleasing. In its day Kaywick must have been a desirable spot in which to live. Given the means to do so I could easily be persuaded to restore it, though finding a suitable way to build a road through the waterlogged hinterland might pose some problems.

The storm's eye moves offshore during the night bringing a return of wind and rain. I am going to need a huge variety of descriptive words for the sea on days like this if I am to avoid forever having to refer to it as pewter or slate. (For some reason 'leaden' gets reserved for sky.) How many shades of grey are there? Don't be surprised if I resort to the obscure, bizarre or even frivolous. I have a feeling that for the next six months at least there is going to be a limited demand on the shades of blue in my palette.

By evening, sky is clearing again with cloud castles reflected in calmer waters. Lowering sun turns them to apricots. It is a fruit with a short shelf life. They become bruised and turn dusky mauve as I watch. Wind has dropped again and there is a hint of frost in the air…

…and it is frost that rimes the fields in the morning. With the still air that always accompanies it, sea is in a reflective mood. Driving north to Sellafirth I discover Basta Voe has captured the surrounding valley's reverse image. Sea's flat surface is a trompe l'œil painting.

Later, in Cullivoe, I walk the high rim of rounded quartz stones above Brough Beach. Millennia of rolling seas aided by the Bluemull's tide race have piled these stones into a massive embankment over fifteen feet wide at the top and nearly

SEA VIEW

as high above the ebb. These smooth bannocks of white granite wink mica that glistens in the bright sun. Though the sea is still calm a long swell is breaking over the Ruggs and the Holm of Brough. It is a reminder of the many hazards seamen face in these waters. Somewhere out there is the dreaded Foustra, made more famous by giving its name to one of Shetland's leading accordion and fiddle bands.

Midweek we travel to Aywick and Gossabrough visiting friends. At Aywick the view from the house is across The Poil to Fetlar, some four miles away. So engaged am I with watching sea breaking on The Poil, I am likely to be thought boorish and inattentive to our hostess. I could cheerfully end my days here in blissful contentment. This is a sea view like no other. By evening the wind has risen to gale force. Tomorrow's view from Aywick will be breathtakingly wild. Noosted into the hillside our gale-strafed house withstands the night's storm as it has hundreds of others. Wind blows through this landscape pretty much unimpeded. It is generally trees that wreak the worst storm damage in other parts of the world and in their absence there is not much the wind can do here but blow and go. By morning the gale has passed. Wind has veered and dropped to a baff. Under the pier quicksilver sea shimmers while further out it shifts indecisively as the fickly breeze bats it hither and thither.

I return to Aywick to hike south along the coast. Sea is peaceful (so much for my prediction of a wild spectacle). Platinum sun lies over the surface, hammered and burnished into a wide sheet, more than sufficient to make a breastplate and shield fit for a king – or a Viking. Turning west round Ness of Queyon towards Otterswick, I pass Black Skerry and come to where 'The White Wife' stands aloof above the banks, not deigning to look upon the cruel sea that held her for so long. She clutches her Bible and gazes heavenward as if hoping to be bodily raised. Her story is recorded on a plaque beside her and relates to the loss of the barque *Bohus*, on 23rd April, 1924. The White Wife was the ship's figurehead and she remained attached to the wreck for five months until September's equinoctial gales broke her free and she came ashore to be salvaged by locals.

A short-cut over Hill of Queyon on the way back takes me past another 'white wife' who glares down at me from the crest. This one, indignantly stamping her feet and snorting, is a shorn sheep. In the hill over half a mile from the coast lie more of those ubiquitous fish boxes. Doubtless, in time, the wind will take them right across the island launching them into the sea once more.

Next day the sea is in one of those indeterminable modes of grey – or should that be moods? I am reminded of a cartoon that appeared in *Punch* (1960 or '61 as I recall): a sombrely-clad draper is standing in the doorway of his dreary 19th century shop holding a dark grey bolt of cloth for inspection. The equally dour-looking customer, dressed all in black and with a black hat in his hand, asks "Have you anything a little less frivolous?"

A suit-length of today's sea might serve his purpose very well though the flecks of dirty white may lead to further hesitancy. My advice would be to come back tomorrow – even this afternoon. There is always new stock coming in.

SEA VIEW

There is a tide in the affairs of men
Which, taken at the flood, leads on to fortune;
Omitted, all the voyage of their life
Is bound in shallows and in miseries.
On such a full sea are we now afloat,
And we must take the current when it serves,
Or lose our ventures.

(*Julius Caesar Act 4, scene 3*)

Looking for subject matter for sketching I visit the old pier in the head of the voe. There is no shortage of material though I will need to return with sunshine to brighten the scene. Here, old derelict houses stand mute, their walls once ringing to the laughter of men and boys long since gone to the whaling or seeking gold in California or Australia. This is a landscape where generations have come and gone for many centuries, leaving their mark in stone before sailing forth. As a seafaring people their tale is often better known by wind and waves than by the soil they briefly tilled.

Wind has boxed the compass in the past 24 hours and is now sou'easterly and freshening. Forecast is for force eight though it is not half that by mid-day.

An inch of fortune is worth a fathom of forecast – so they say. Forecasting in this part of the world is far from an exact science. Admittedly the geography, when set against the forces of nature, must make accurate forecasting extremely difficult hereabouts. By comparison the relationship between my old home of Tasmania and the many hundreds of miles of open sea to its west (where most of the weather comes from) makes forecasting much easier there. Even a total ignoramus such as I could fairly accurately predict outcomes when confronted with a chart showing isobars and barometric pressures.

How quickly things can change. A boat has recently left the pier spreading silver pleats on black calm water. It is 8am. Nothing is moving… correction, a skein of grey-lag geese crosses the sky and a hooded crow flaps languorously to a chimney top on a roofless ruin. Sun is already in my valley, winking in windows to wake sleepyheads. The clock ticks into my silence telling me I must not waste this day and so I set out for The Herra on Whalfirth, which is a four-mile-long sea arm that almost cuts through the middle of Yell to link up with Mid Yell Voe.

Dr Harry Taylor, in his account of life as a GP in Yell at the beginning of last century (*A Shetland Parish Doctor*, Shetland News; 1948), makes an interesting observation regarding the proximity of these voes to one another, suggesting that it "would not be an expensive undertaking" to connect the two by means of a narrow channel. (They are separated by less than half a mile.) According to Taylor, the resulting tidal force "would produce abundant water power for the generation of electricity". As to whether the idea is feasible or has any merit is a matter for the experts but it might be worth exploring.

The Herra is halfway down the west side of Whalfirth; a sprinkling of houses in what was once a sizeable community. Walking north to the mouth of the firth

SEA VIEW

I pass remnants of long-forgotten crofts – seven or eight tumbled heaps of stone where, in centuries gone by, men and women eked out a living or, more probably, struggled to survive.

Climbing to the high ground of Virdi Field, Stany Hill and Green Hill, to escape the sodden moor, I am rewarded with distant views to North Mainland and Saxa Vord on Unst. In steep banks below me sheep are grazing the short grass, climbing surefooted as wild goats into clefts and gullies in search of the best pickings. A jagged white rock thrusts up from the sea like a giant's molar reflecting early morning sun *(see photo page iii)*. As I traverse the cliff top the changing angles offer several spectacular photographs. I am lucky to have captured the light as cloud is swiftly building and the best of the day is spent.

Taking a beeline back to the car I risk wet feet crossing chortling burns, every footfall a noisy squelch.

A late start has me heading for the entrance to Mid Yell Voe then south round the headland towards Vatsetter. I make heavy going of it on a steep slope of long grass and sphagnum moss. Rabbits scurry before me bringing to mind a nonsense yarn read by a somewhat eccentric English master I studied under when I was a schoolboy. It was a hot Friday afternoon with all the classroom windows open – the last session of the week and no one (including the master) inclined to serious study. And so he read us this crazy story about a bloke named Ironbark Bill who lived in Outback Australia where the hills were so steep all the rabbits had developed two short legs on one side and two long legs on the other resulting in their only being able to run round the hills in one direction. Ironbark Bill put a bend in his gun and set off round a hill in the opposite direction having trained his dog to run round at a lower level with an open sack in his mouth. One shot could skittle up to a dozen rabbits with Ironbark's dog retrieving the tumbling carcases.

It is over 55 years since I heard that story and I admit to my memory being a bit vague on detail. In all probability I have changed it beyond recognition and therefore am not likely to be in breach of copyright. Hope not, anyway. Now I am making a careful study of these local rabbits to see if they have begun to genetically mutate in order to better traverse this confounded slope which is causing my ankles to ache. It is a relief to reach the sandy ayre at Vatsetter and take the road back to Mid Yell.

Out once more, my way is south again having first crossed a sodden moor below Loch of Vatsetter to reach the coast. Visibility is poor and deteriorating as the afternoon wears on. I pass two mounds smoothly topped with moss and devoid of any other vegetation. Being in fanciful mood I decide they are Trow Hadds, though I am unable to detect an entrance to either (not surprising as Trows are skilled at hiding them). It is as well I am not a fiddle player or I might be spirited away to make music for these mischievous lovers of entertainment who have been known to keep a good musician for up to a year before releasing him. Reaching the cliffs near The Poil, I come on ruins of a house named Stoal. Later I am told the house was inhabited about fifty years ago. It is roofless now and there is little to distinguish it from other ruins that have been empty for hundreds of years. Proximity to cliffs and deep geos cause me to wonder at the obvious dangers of raising a family in such a place. This is a wild, lonely spot where sea is master. It is also a hauntingly beautiful location which I feel compelled to visit again as soon as possible.

By morning the sea has turned to navy blue with white trimmings. Landward there is some activity going on and my nose is beginning to twitch with curiosity. A red-capped chatterer flits past the house followed by a tartan-throated greatcoat. Nearby two double-breasted long shanks are combing the shrubbery, both have shouldered tripods and all the paraphernalia needed for recording their sightings. The twitchers have come. I go out for a gander and a chat. It appears a taiga flycatcher was sighted in the vicinity recently and a Hornemann's Arctic redpoll is thought to be hereabouts also. No less than seventeen different species of uncommon birds (some rarely seen in Shetland) have been sighted this week – mostly in Yell and Fetlar. No wonder the twitchers are out in force. This is exciting stuff.

Okay, maybe it doesn't excite everyone but no one can deny that this is one of Shetland's greatest attractions and I intend keeping the binoculars to hand. If the red-capped chatterer returns I might try for a photograph and send it to *International Bird Fanciers Magazine*. I wouldn't mind betting this green-wellied, Barbour-backed species is a first for Shetland.

Returning (as planned) to Aywick, I walk out to the ruin of Stoal where there are also remains of a prehistoric fort. The last occupant of Stoal was Jessie Mouat, schoolteacher at Aywick for over 40 years. Jessie vacated the house in the early 1950s, after which it soon became the ruin we see today. I am drawn to wondering (as I did on my previous visit) at the rapidity with which this house has lost every vestige or sign of habitation. How easily the moor covers all trace of man. How soon the stones of centuries fall and are forgotten.

And what of us? Can we hope to endure in people's memories a little longer or are we truly dust and destined to as quickly go the way of our homes?

We travel north to Unst on a sightseeing tour. The landscape is dotted with twitchers hoping for a sight of one or other of the latest avian arrivals. Yesterday's *Shetland Times* reported the season's first whooper swans, down from arctic regions for their winter sojourn in Shetland. A pair has been sighted at Uyeasound. Already many more have arrived and soon lochs throughout Shetland will be dotted with them. Nearby, a stately and aloof pair of mute swans is, for me, a more exciting discovery. Mutes are relative newcomers to Shetland and these are my first sighting. Am I now becoming a twitcher?

On a day of calm weather, sea defers to spectacular cliffs for first attention, though in this part of the world the reverse is more generally the case, as is clearly witnessed by the dramatic coastline where stacks, arches, caves and deep geos abound. This has been a surfeit-of-sea day.

Wind shifting to the north brings a late change to an otherwise lousy day. By 3pm sunshine sparkles on the voe and we venture out to sing *All Things Bright and Beautiful* at the late service in the kirk. We should be so lucky!

A small boy in orange wellies and green luminescent parka is walking back and fore in the ebb towing a plastic boat on a string. His fingers must be freezing in the nipsiccar northerly wind. Lapping waves rock his boat. Does he dream of going to sea when he becomes a man?

Monday brings a near perfect autumn day. By early afternoon I escape tedious chores to catch the best of it, parking the car at Harkland in West Yell and heading north. Though the sea is comparatively calm, a light swell is woofing and frothing in deep geos. A glimpse of white on a landlocked loch temporarily diverts me inland. Fourteen whooper swans raise nervous heads as I appear on the skyline.

They are unwilling to share their space with me, making a hasty and scarcely dignified retreat. Snipe are similarly disposed, whirring out of the heather in exaggerated alarm to set inquisitive rabbits scurrying. Sun breaks from cloud, luring me back to the coast as it casts away shadows and throws the scene into sharp relief. I'm drawn to a flat-topped headland connected to the cliff-face by a narrow land-bridge and known as The Birrier. A similar outcrop with the same

name can be found on the opposite side of Yell, near Vatsetter. It seems the name derives from the characteristics of these features but I am unable to determine the exact meaning.

A large rock known as 'The old wife of The Birrier' stands at the edge of the cliff by the land-bridge and seems to warn against any foolhardiness in her domain. The lure of an ancient settlement on top of The Birrier is not enough to tempt me. This is a dangerous place and not for the faint-hearted. I decide to give it a miss and head home. The southerly breeze is a warm caress. It is a day to remember.

A south-easterly buster is whipping the voe into frenzy. Out to sea breakers roll in regimented formation, while here behind the headland flans hit the surface then skate across the voe forming patterns of light and shade. When my grandfather raised his top hat the pleated grey silk lining shimmered like quicksilver. This is the image of today's sea though I am disinclined to raise my hat to it. Weather remains rough all day "makkin a skaar a weet" (creating a little rain) as Shetlanders say in classic understatement.

Housebound, I turn to yarn-spinning…

Lost & Found

It was the glint of sun on glass that caught the boy's attention. He frequently took this longer way home from school, detouring along Levenwick Beach in the hope of finding something interesting. Wind had been in the southern quarter for a couple of days and this was the direction which best favoured his chances of making a find. Flotsam was regularly sucked in on back-surge round The Bulwark to make its way up to the crescent of sand where he now stood wet-footed in the ebb. He had listened to his grandfather tell tales of seamen putting messages in bottles then throwing them overboard in far off oceans, and how great currents such as the Gulf Stream picked them up and carried them round the world.

Local fishermen occasionally launched message bottles which sometimes turned up on nearby beaches having travelled less than a couple of miles. The boy hoped it was not one of these as he squatted down, digging into the firm sand with both hands. He could feel the excitement beginning to course in his veins as he saw that it was indeed a bottle and that it was intact and sealed with a cork. He had found plenty bottles before – usually plastic ones or ones half full of water, bobbing and nodding in the ebb like drunken marionettes. This one was different. He gingerly prised it out of the wet sand, lifting it up to the light and attempting to peer through the heavily stained glass. It was practically opaque from frequent abrasive contact with countless other beaches it had visited during its long journey. This was no local fisherman's offering.

There seemed to be a piece of paper inside but it was difficult to be sure. The cork had broken off, leaving a stub firmly jammed inside the neck. The boy was tempted to smash his find on a rock. Very nearly did, but something held him back. Later on, he would tell his best friend that he was "sort of scared."

"How do you mean?" his friend had asked.

SEA VIEW

"Don't rightly know. It was like... you know... maybe there was something spooky in the bottle..." then he shrugged. "Anyway, I just wanted mam or dad to be there when I opened it – just in case," and he had shrugged a second time.

"Just as well you did," his friend had remarked, his eyes getting big and round as he recalled the outcome. "Holy moly, no one would've believed you if you'd come walking in with __that__ message and said you'd found it in a bottle!"

And he had a point (as you may judge for yourself).

The partially obliterated and faded message was on a tightly rolled piece of rust-stained, torn linen, which the boy's father had removed from the bottle. It related to an event they all knew about from history lessons at school.

Going from hand to hand, this is what they read:

'Mary Celeste... 37° N, 25° W ..., Dec... 1872... all hands except...'

When it comes to sea views, they don't come much better than Lerwick's – even on a day like this one which is as grey as the stonewalled buildings that overlook the docks. Waves lapping or crashing on empty coastal reaches are one thing. The hustle and bustle of a working port is something else altogether.

When we top the hill above Gremista for a first glimpse of the harbour the Skerries ferry is heading out of Bressay Sound, and NorthLink's passengers are making a late disembarkation at Holmsgarth after a wild North Sea passage up from Aberdeen.

At Victoria Pier, below the Market Cross, a sleek naval vessel lies alongside two Irish pelagic trawlers. There is a seismic ship from the Bahamas; a dive support vessel from Liberia and another from Panama; a reefer from Nassau and a supply ship from India – a typical United Nations line-up. Needless-to-say, most of this is not immediately apparent but, it being Friday, *The Shetland Times* has the gist of it for our edification. *Fishing/Marine* news and the *Weather Report* generally share a page and are essential reading for Shetlanders who all have a view to the sea if not a Sea View.

A visit to Lerwick always includes a 'sassermaet' roll. You will readily discern the 'maet' bit. The inside-out spelling is merely a phonetic representation of how Shetlanders pronounce the word. However, it's anyone's guess what *sort* of meat goes into the mix. All sorts, I suspect. Better not to ask. This leaves us with 'sasser' (not 'saucer' as some misguided Sassenachs would have us believe). The word has its origins in the old Norn language that was once spoken in Shetland. It started out as 'saks' (chopped) but got corrupted along the way, and if you think that simply means minced, think again. There is more to the concoction than minced meat and all of it has to do with spices. Cast your eye over the list and you will get an inkling of what I am driving at – mace, cloves, ginger, allspice, cinnamon, black pepper, white pepper, Jamaica pepper – enough to make your eyes water. And then there is salt. The recipe in front of me stipulates six ounces to 12 lbs of meat. Oh yes, this stuff is manufactured in bulk and is potent. The recipe goes back to long before the terms 'shelf-life' and 'use-by-date' were invented (hence the heavy-handed salting). The end product is spicy and salty. It is Shetland's favourite dish and no day trip from the provinces to the capital is complete without a sassermaet roll (generally washed down with copious quantities of well-stewed tea). Every café and restaurant in Lerwick has sassermaet on its menu. It is Shetland's answer to a MacDonald's burger and, incidentally, it would not surprise me in the least to discover that the only reason MacDonald's have failed to colonise Lerwick is that they are afraid to go head-to-head against sassermaet, because they know they can never win. In Shetland, sassermaet rules OK.

With winter still over a month away, I am beginning to get an inkling of what is to come. After three days of sou-easterly winds, Stoal Reef at Aywick is taking a pounding. This is a view I will keep returning to. It is a scene worthy of a large canvas and the hand of an artist. In the absence of both I will have to unpack my pastels and make some sort of an attempt to capture it. At nightfall, wind rises to gale force. It is a real chimney howler. Sea rocks my island home.

Thankfully, it has blown itself out by morning though the voe still carries its aftermath and the beach-head is covered in foam.

Here comes the sun, sweeping a broad scythe over the hills to lay down a windrow of cheer and warmth. After a three-day absence, it is a most welcome return of a good friend, however brief the visit may prove to be. *Conquest* is delivering her catch into the back of an articulated truck, shiny and bloodied white-bellied salmon sliding down the chute, their journey to a cordon bleu chef begun. Best if diners do not think too much about the process even if knowledge might help explain price. Car and house windows are rimed with salt from the gale-driven sea.

I head for the East Yell Birrier – no distance down the road. The tramp round White Hill of Vatsetter takes me past beaches piled with fresh seaweed. Sheep are in the ebb eating this nutrient-rich supplement to their diet. It is one of the things that gives the distinctive 'gamey' flavour to Shetland mutton. Chefs are advised to go easy on the rosemary and other seasonings in order not to mask this readymade *bouquet garni*.

A natural arch connects the Birrier to the mainland. The crossing is narrow and probably a step too far. I come on remnants of what might once have been a monastic dwelling similar to ones on West Yell Birrier. There are many such places around Shetland along with remains of hermit's cells in some cliffs. It is difficult to imagine what might have attracted people to such exposed sites and more difficult still to imagine how they survived. Rather them than me.

Etched by a passing boat, multiple black and silver lines are curving into the voe, advancing through a pliant sea. I have watched several vessels come and go over the last half hour, each leaving its signature to resonate across the water. Between times the surface looks like tightly stretched latex that is being punctured by diving gulls, the holes slowly expanding – runs in a silk stocking – only to be invisibly mended moments later. Each time I look out the scene is being repeated. Am I watching a video loop? No, shifting light and zephyr breezes are constantly making subtle changes while tide is ebbing. In a few hours it will all be quite different. This is the joy of a sea view.

SEA VIEW

Later that night Caolum lay in his own bed and listened to the sough of the ocean as it came and went on the beach like an exhausted beast laboriously inhaling and exhaling after a long journey. Whether as now, in the rhythmic pattern characterised by calm weather, or in the discordant crash of a storm, it was always the sea that spoke to him first and last every day. He knew all its songs by heart; knew when the moder-dy crested and when she reached the shore; knew the cries of her many children. And when all was calm under a full moon he might leave his bed and sit by the earth-stone to listen for the sound of lost souls far out in the deep or to whispered tales told along the rim of the ebb by crabs waiting to receive the dead. Like beads in a priest's rosary, the sea contained all the theosophy needed to bestow peace to his heart and sleep to his tired body. (Excerpt from an unpublished manuscript titled *The Ninian Plate*)

Wind is south-westerly and battering squarely on my door. Not being sufficiently experienced in estimating its speed I ask Ivor, a retired fisherman. "Force seven," he says without hesitation.

I have already observed how little the wind affects land in these parts and from inside the house it can be difficult to tell how strong it is without some visible sign. However, while land may be passively indifferent and give nothing away, vulnerable sea is entirely at wind's mercy. With a sea view it is another story as every guff, gooster or gale is recorded on the surface – wind's saga writ large and easily read by those who know the language.

Sea is as ruffled feathers under a misty dome. Here and there, zigzag patches of oily calm break the monotony though what causes them is a mystery to me. Not oil. Fluky shifts of air, I suspect. At 3pm, when I take a short stroll along the waterfront, the tide is at its lowest ebb. An exposed rock looks like a walrus complete with seaweed whiskers. Desultory surf snores and sighs through pulverised storm wrack. The once pristine beach is littered with debris. Tide's late shift will either take it away or tidy it into orderly windrows where ebb-eaters can forage and beachcombers extract the odd find. By nightfall, wind is rising again.

Today massive cloud galleons sail out of the west fully laden and spanking across the sky; main, topsails and topgallants billowing. High above them cirrus sheets are stretched to dry, glistening in early morning light. Sea is a bit player today, content to reflect from calming backwaters on the high drama heralding the day. Its time will come…

… never a truer word! Force nine. Air is full of flying spray, a fine mist being driven far inshore. All along the voe's west shore a lacy frill of white shreds itself against the sea wall; its tattered remnants stringing over the graveyard's rooted stones, several of which carry epitaphs of men lost at sea. Restless sea, come to wake the dead.

At full tide, waves are breaking across the pier depositing sand (the links) and dulse outside Linkshouse shop door. No need to leave the house for today's sea view…

SEA VIEW

...but leave it I do, heading south for even more spectacular coastal views. Aywick (The Poil) and Otterswick (Black Skerry) are receiving the full brunt of this storm. Outside the car it is hard to stand. Photography is impossible due to flying spray and lashing rain. Inside it is a case of trying to synchronise photos with windscreen wipers and hoping for a brief shaft of sunlight between the clouds. Some hope! From the comfort of a heated car, I watch the White Wife

SEA VIEW

as she stands in defiance of everything the elements can throw at her. Must she forever be reminded of that fateful day when her ship foundered and she failed to protect her charges?

Under pale apricot cloud, the surface of the voe has a luminescent glow. Close inshore its pleated viscosity resembles mercury. Today's sea is soothing the rocks that it so mercilessly punished yesterday. Peace has been restored, though it appears to be an uneasy truce. Out beyond the headland white fangs are still being bared, while closer to hand the beach is a child's paradise. Every tide may potentially bring new treasure and any wave can deliver a surprise. The sandy ayre out of which juts Mid Yell pier is a favourite spot for local bairns who happily brave all weathers to paddle and bob like oystercatchers with every bit as much expectation of success. Add a dog to the equation and the excitement is multiplied ten-fold. Dogs love retrieving objects thrown into the sea and seem to take particular delight in then shaking water and sand all over their owners. Today's criss-crossed footprints in the sand tell of fun and games between bairns and a dog. Though the players are gone, the echo of their laughter lingers in the waves. When tide cleans the slate it may leave a gift for tomorrow's children.

In the night, while others sleep, I lie and listen to the sea. Spawned out of an unlikely coupling of hemispheres, suckled first by glaciers and icebergs then by monsoons and mighty rivers, it is set adrift to wander round the globe forever. It is by turn a delinquent child, a ravishing beauty, an alluring seducer, a restless beast, an angry tyrant and a tired old man. Tonight (to judge by its sonorous breathing), it is the latter come seeking a sympathetic shore on which to lie awhile and rest.

> *Break, break, break*
> *At the foot of the crags O Sea!*
> *But the tender grace of a day that is dead*
> *Will never come back to me.*
> (Alfred, Lord Tennyson)

I am slowly getting used to the low altitude of sun at this latitude. It scarcely makes it out of sky's southern quarter at this time of year. Only 2pm, but already I have left it a little late to start my planned hike. In bright sunshine, I head west to Ness of Sound where a lovely little whitewashed cottage sits above a shingle ayre. Like a frightened rabbit at its bolt-hole, the sun dodges for cloud cover every time I take out my camera. A couple of quick snapshots and it bolts for keeps. I cross the ness for a view over Yell Sound. On the mossy crest are remains of peat banks, the working face no longer clean-cut but collapsed and worn ragged with the passage of time. It must be many years since anyone came here to cut out their fuel. The bank is a hollow square, the lower level (known as the greff) having long since grown over again. It is possible to calculate the number of years the bank has been worked by counting the slightly furrowed character of the greff. I count fifty but it could well be more. Winter fuel for a couple of

SEA VIEW

generations. Rarely do you see any open peat banks in Shetland today, despite the high cost of oil and electricity. It seems everyone has better things to do.

I continue down to another working face – the sea cliffs of Yell Sound. This is a work in progress, though being a calm day there is not much going on. I can hear the glop and splat of sea as it mutters in deep caverns below me, no doubt impatient to be getting on with the job – this one measured in millions of years. Geos bear the harrowing scars of sea's relentless chiselling. A squall is heading my way. It's a race to the car. Squall wins. I am drenched. Nor is there any cheer to be had from the rainbow.

On a day when the sun fails to make an appearance, sunset is scarcely noteworthy or notable other than to mark the gradual coming of night. By 4pm the sky begins to darken so presumably the event has taken place. More to the point, wind is rising. It is time for birds and beasts to look for shelter and all little boats had better make for port.

It will not be a night to be on the high seas. And I do mean high. "We're in for a rough night," the man said, "best get home before it worsens."

I take his advice. Already I can hear ominous sounds – groaning, moaning, wailing. A black sea is heaving restlessly, an unbroken stallion chafing at the bit…

… yet in the morning I wake to virtual calm. What became of the storm? Sea is laughing, though there is little to laugh about from its perspective – lying on its back looking at a glowering sky filled to overflowing with rain clouds.

A hooded crow is dropping a mussel on the road, trying to crack the shell. In a nearby field a second crow is watching the proceedings with interest. After several attempts, which involve carrying the shell to a height of fifty feet or so and always directly above the road's hard surface, the mussel is beginning to look the worse for wear. Persistence is about to be rewarded. Now with typical corvine-cunning the second bird flies to within a couple of crow-steps of the action. This creates a dilemma for the industrious one. If he attempts one last drop the interloper will snatch the prize. Now what? A bit of posturing on both parts achieves nothing. You can imagine the shell-owner muttering, "Stone the crows!" Attempts to drive off the interloper are unsuccessful and eventually the first crow picks up his snack-pack and flies off in disgust. Talk about a couple of wily old birds!

And NOW the storm arrives! Actually, it arrived in the middle of the night, a bull in a china shop bellowing fit to wake the dead. One minute a starry sky and peaceful sea then all hell is let loose. I lie awake, listening to it building to a crescendo. A banshee would cause less disturbance – make that a whole host of banshees. And now, in the morning… well, put it this way, it doesn't make a blind bit of difference whether I draw back the curtains or leave them closed. The outlook is basically the same – which is to say there isn't any outlook. Storms like these bring everything to a halt in the islands. No ferries running. No planes flying. No mail. What's needed on a day like this is a good book.

SEA VIEW

It has been said "if you don't like the weather in Shetland, wait a minute and it will change". How true. I have scarcely finished writing the above paragraph when ragged holes begin to appear in the cloud cover. A few minutes later and the whole box and dice is being dragged away, for all the world like sliding open a coupé roof hatch to reveal blue sky above. It's a whole new day. We make a snap decision to catch the next ferry (oh yes, they are running again, along with everything else) and in little over an hour we are in Lerwick. Don't get me wrong; it isn't any sort of day to write home about. 'Indifferent' is about the best I can say of it. The thing is, when you decide to take a trip to Lerwick from one of the northern isles – or any of the more remote parts of Shetland for that matter, you don't let the weather get in the way, or get you down. There is too much else to occupy your mind and at the back of it is the thought that you have that return ferry to catch (or that long drive through the hills on a single track road in the dark).

Lerwick is Shetland's main business centre and most activity revolves round it. In my case this means spending time mooning about the harbour taking in all the sights and sounds, soaking up the atmosphere and working up an appetite for fish and chips while my better half rushes about doing the shopping, banking and whatever else can't wait till another (brighter) day. It is not that I am selfish (I nearly wrote shellfish) but as anyone worth his salt will tell you, if a job is worth doing its worth doing well.

Today's sea is the underbelly of a mackerel; a glittering prize, supposing you could hold it. But it cannot be captured or tamed and in the too-soon absence of sun it will turn lacklustre once more. Let me keep it before my glad eyes a little longer. Beyond the hills, cloud battalions are marshalling again. Shall I whistle up the wind and drive them away? No need. Barometric pressure has spun my wheel of fortune. By noon the sky is clear. Every last segment of cloud turned tail and fled. And at nightfall it is sky's turn to glitter, evoking a winking response from the sea.

I hear tell of a boy, not twelve years old, who was killed when he fell from cliffs at the Ness of Lussetter. It happened over 60 years ago yet his pal who was playing with him that day remembers it as though it was yesterday. I look in the graveyard for a stone bearing the boy's name but cannot find one. I do not ask for further details, not wanting to see pain rekindled in the eyes of the old man. It is enough that he has had to live with this disaster all his life. How many others carry associated memories of loved ones taken by the sea? I have already found too many headstones with the inscription 'Lost at Sea'. It is a black thread that weaves through the fabric of a seafaring community.

From my front window I can see the road north; the road that trails up through brown moors bringing traffic from one ferry to the next on a journey to Shetland's most northerly island of Unst. From here, it is a thin black pencil line curving away beyond the far side of the voe. While I'm watching sea, hoping to read its mood for the day, I'm distracted by cars winding their way through the

SEA VIEW

hills. A glide of headlights in the dull, early morning; weaving fireflies drifting in and out of mist. You may know by this diversion from the main game that sea is not in contention. It is huffing and heaving – "oobin and takin on" as a Shetlander might say when describing a recalcitrant child moaning around the house. Best ignored. There *is* some surface action however. A small fishing boat is circling in the middle of the voe with two or three men in yellow oilskins busy about the deck as they gut their catch. How do I know what they are doing? The frenzied flock of gulls astern is a dead giveaway.

A short while later my attention is drawn to some activity at the pier. A barge with a crane has arrived to deliver a small white van. While the skipper holds the vessel bow-on to the pier by means of propeller-power, his crane operator slings the van ashore. Five minutes, no more, and they're off. Meanwhile the usual flotilla of fishing boats fuss back and fore through the voe. Never a dull moment. And fish for tea.

Seven lights equally spaced along the pier cast seven shimmering amber paths across black water like spilled ribbons of whisky. And in my window a bridge of seven candles reflects in the glass, shining out and making the raindrops glow like chips of other amber. Homecoming fishermen may be cheered by the sight before heading to their own lighted windows and a well-earned dram.

Antique silver-plate worn through to copper and burnished until it gleams. This is my sea view at sunrise. I drive to West Sandwick and end up at the beach where, despite calm weather, substantial surf is breaking. This is a place to visit on a fine summer day (or at sunset). I can foresee me coming again and again. If I had my pick of houses in this place it would be hard to choose as most have exceptional views over Yell Sound. It is worth noting how well the old-timers chose the sites on which to build their houses and how well those old houses fit into the landscape. Whitewashed and trig above their well-kept rigs, they are entirely pleasing to the eye. The modern-day versions cannot hold a candle to them.

At 9pm, I take a stroll down to the pier. It is a black night with a touch of frost in the air. Anthracite sea gleams coldly despite being dotted with amber braziers of reflected light from nearby houses. Yesterday's barge lies moored alongside. I note the name – *Bagheera*. It seems an improbable moniker for a barge, even if the orange crane fixed to its deck looks vaguely like a crouching tiger and there is a veritable jungle of junk surrounding it. No doubt Rudyard Kipling would be amused.

On a cold, grey day, I walk up beside the burn at the head of Basta Voe in company with Ian. Though this is quite a small and seemingly insignificant stream, yet it is known to provide good fishing in season as both salmon and sea trout travel up to the large loch of Gossa Water to spawn.

Ian tells me of a boyhood experience when he hooked a salmon only to have it make off down the voe with the entire contents of his fishing reel. "I tried to increase tension on the line which was 10lbs breaking strain or thereabouts. I

SEA VIEW

was attempting to slow its run by using my fingers but the fish was too strong, I couldn't stop it. When the reel ran out the line snapped. Ping! It took the lot. I went round the top of the voe to get my other rod and while I was doing so my brother hooked another one. He was determined not to let the same thing happen so he screwed up the tension on his reel. Ping! He'd tightened it too much!" The memory of it evokes a wry grin from Ian. How is it that fishermen always seem to relish telling tales of the ones that get away?

Looking into the black water winding through the valley, I'm thinking this is definitely a burn to visit next summer. I am even selecting likely pools in which to cast a fly. The long arm of Basta Voe is like a funnel. Fish returning here will get a taste of their birth stream long before they reach it and will come unerringly home with quickened pulse and powerful instinct. I'll be waiting.

I'm out before the sun, heading for West Sandwick in the expectation of bright skies within the hour. Sea is pounding the rocks. I can hear it before I see it and am reminded of stories of the First World War, when the noise of heavy artillery bombardments on the Western Front could be heard from miles behind the lines. I fancy the 'crump' and 'thud' I am now hearing may be a similar sound. It is awesome.

Turning south, I make for a rocky headland where there is supposed to be the remains of a broch. Reaching the spot, I abruptly come to a halt. An otter is standing in the ebb amongst seaweed. He is perhaps twenty yards from me. This is my first sighting since beginning this account though I have been hoping to come on one almost every day. He has his back to me and so far appears unaware of my presence. An adult male, I guess – handsome looking fellow too, sleek and well fed. I slowly open my camera bag, hoping for a photograph. Suddenly he looks back over his shoulder and on seeing me runs quickly up the bank and down a rabbit burrow. A moment later a very indignant looking rabbit comes flying out of the same hole, no doubt having been given a sharp nip for choosing to be in the wrong place at the wrong time. In the excitement, I forget all about looking for the broch.

Sun is in the clear now and likely to remain so for three or four hours. Mica chips in veins of white quartz glisten amongst the grey rocks. I continue south to the head of the ness, climbing onto high ground for a wider view across Southladie Voe. Only at the very top under stunted heather is the ground reasonably firm. Everywhere else is a veritable bog with each step squishing and sucking noisily. Pigs at a trough would make less noise. Stealth is not an option as I return downwind to where the otter appeared earlier. I am not surprised that it is nowhere to be seen. Never mind, there are other photo opportunities in the vicinity of West Sandwick beach and I spend a productive half hour before heading home.

On another fine and calm day I walk to the marina at the head of Mid Yell voe. At the nearby pier, the little flotilla that supplies the fish factory is lying reflecting on its day of rest.

SEA VIEW

By afternoon, frothy clouds are bustling up over the horizon and spilling across blue sky much as yesterday's waves broke upon the beach, the difference being that clouds meet with no resistance. Sea will always find a barrier to beat its fists upon.

Overnight the heavens clear, and the following morning is frosty. Though the day starts in blue skies, cloud is not long in making an appearance. Nevertheless, it is sufficiently bright to lure me in search of some coastal photography. I head for North Yell and the Ness of Houlland. Once again, I am astounded at the way sheep will climb down extremely hazardous paths in order to reach inaccessible tufts of grass on cliff ledges. As winter wears on and fodder becomes less abundant, sheep will take ever-greater risks in this regard. Crofters have attempted to fence off the worst hazards but the diminutive Shetland sheep are not easily put off and invariably seem to find a way through. Inevitably, some will fall to their death. Where sheep cannot go rabbits still can – and do. They frequent the cliff face with the same nonchalance as the gulls. If they fall, will that constitute pie in the sky?

Cliff formation in this region resembles buttresses on a fortress – or I might compare them to an ogre's gap-tooth snarl as he contemplates biting a chunk out of the Blue Mull across the way on Unst. Local folklore tells of argumentative giants heaving rocks at one another hereabouts. Perhaps this is what knocked the teeth out. Folklore aside, there can be little doubting that sea has wrought havoc upon the land here for millions of year, tearing it asunder and pulverising it mercilessly to create one of Shetland's largest and loveliest beaches – the Sands of Breckon *(see photo page ii)*. The contrast between this wide strand with its extended dunes covered in bent and the nearby ominously dark fissures and towering cliffs could not be greater. It comes as no surprise to discover that medieval Christians were attracted to this place and that it has remained the preferred burial ground for centuries of North Yell inhabitants. There are few more picturesque spots in Shetland.

My ear is tuned to the cry of gulls that are so much a part of everyday life by the sea. Sometimes it is a raucous flock squabbling over scraps thrown from

SEA VIEW

fishing boats, and sometimes the plaintive cry of a lone bird seeking company or discontentedly mewing in the manner of an agitator holding forth at a protest rally. To the untrained ear it is all just so much noise, though doubtless the language of gulls makes sense to the individual species. At times, they seem to prefer company, congregating in large flocks as though waiting for something momentous to happen. Then again, I many times see an individual gull standing alone or perhaps pottering about with no apparent intent at the sea's edge. Some cut solitary figures on rocks – sentinels of the sea, or float motionless like water-lilies, looking all the more forlorn for the vast expanse of ocean surrounding them.

The large glaucous and great black-backed gulls when seen alone present an impression of aloofness or disdain, turning their backs as you pass while never ceasing to keep a cold eye on proceedings. Kittiwakes and other smaller gulls roam through the sky in characteristic artistry of flight, dainty as swallows.

From time to time, outflow from the crab-factory includes tasty morsels that bring screaming flocks wheeling into the voe, diving and jostling, swearing fit to turn the air blue and pecking one another viciously. Talk about disturbing the peace!

When fighting and feeding are over gulls settle in seemingly random groups on the sea to form intriguing white patterns on grey slate. Puzzles for the cryptologists to decipher, though they might find themselves gulled.

Sea covers approximately 70 per cent of the world's surface and more than half of it is over 9,000 feet deep. If I tip a bucket of water off the end of the pier, and were I able to manipulate the molecules to prevent them dispersing or interchanging with others around them, they might potentially be carried by wind, tide, salinity differences, Coriolis force (whatever that is), streams, climate change and much else, to circumnavigate the globe, sinking to the blackest depths where unknown monsters lurk, then rising again to ride rogue waves; pass through the Bermuda Triangle, Straits of Malacca, North West Passage, Doldrums, Barrier Reef, Hudson Bay and a million other places, before returning again in another millennium with enough stories to fill a library.

Meanwhile, within the time-span of a tide, the wind goes from zero to 70mph. Sea has gone from calm to seething in the twinkling of an eye. Is this a case of bipolar disorder or merely polar proximity? What is the prognosis? Pour oil on troubled waters or rub salt into the wound? Will a sea change affect a cure?

In the blink of sunshine that is to be my ration for today, I scurry round to North-a-Voe hoping for a glimpse of something to write about. In a sheltered corner appropriately named *Seafield*, where the road skirts the sea and crumbling ruins overlook an old pier, two seals have hauled themselves out on seaweed-covered rocks. Presumably, they too are hoping to make the most of the weak sunshine. This one-time fishing station is a place steeped in history. I can practically hear the tumbled stones echoing voices of long-gone seafarers who have set out from this place to seek their fortune.

SEA VIEW

Shards of showers stretch obliquely between sky and sea. They are the angry brush strokes of a frustrated artist whose earlier canvas did not come up to expectations. At my feet is the first seasonal fall of snow – a sprinkle only, but with the ground already cold it will be slow to melt. Sea has a correspondingly icy appearance. Figuratively speaking one might skate its surface though in fact its temperature will not have diminished one iota. Gulls may well consider it a desirable place to be at the moment – warmer than anywhere else.

In a previous life, I used to design knitting patterns. The following is one I named *Sea Change (see photo page iii)*. It is a traditional Shetland pattern to which I have given a make-over. For well over a century this type of scarf was knitted using fine hand-spun yarn in natural shades of wool. In more recent times, 2-ply lace yarn in pastel shades has been favoured, generally in regulated bands of colour. My pattern is inspired by reflections in the sea and in the same way as such reflections may change with a shift of light, so the colours are used in a free-form way. My intention is not to dictate a pattern but to encourage creativity. Contrary to tradition, I used Shetland 4-ply (jumper yarn) as there are over 150 shades to choose from. I also used larger than usual needles (5 mm) for a more open 'relaxed' look. The resultant scarf will have excellent thermal properties.

SEA VIEW

The yarn can be obtained from Jamieson & Smith Ltd (Wool Broker, Lerwick; www.shetlandwoolbrokers.co.uk) where their wide selection of heathery marls make it possible to create exquisite and subtle effects

Knitting instructions: Choose 5 or 6 complementary shades of 4-ply Shetland yarn. With 5mm needles cast on 53 sts. Knit 4, knit 2 together, knit 2, yarn forward, knit 1, *yarn forward, knit 4, slip 1, knit 2 together, pass slipped stitch over, knit 4, yarn forward, knit 1*; repeat between * 2 more times; yarn forward, knit 2, knit 2 together, knit 4. Repeat every row the same, changing colours as preferred in random bands of between 1 and 5 rows. Knit to approximately 75cm, leaving stitches on a holder. Knit a second piece to the same length though not necessarily in the same colour sequence. Return first work to a needle and graft both pieces together (see below). The finished scarf will be greatly improved by washing and pinning out under tension on a flat surface.

Grafting instructions: Place the two pieces to be grafted one above the other with the needles parallel and facing right (left for left-handers). Thread a length of same colour wool on a blunt needle (hereafter referred to as GN (grafting needle). Proceed as follows: Insert GN as if for knitting into the 1st stitch of the lower needle and slip the stitch off the needle. Insert GN as if for purling into the 2nd stitch of same needle, drawing the wool through and leaving stitch on the needle. Take GN under the lower needle and insert as if for purling into 1st stitch of top needle drawing wool through and slipping stitch off needle. Insert GN as if for knitting in 2nd stitch of top needle drawing wool through and leaving stitch on needle. Bring GN forward under needle and repeat from the beginning.

It is a beautiful evening and the low angle of sunlight is brightly illuminating solans (gannets) wheeling and diving about a mile off shore. Such acrobatics are worthy of the Bolshoi Ballet.

Already a season has come and gone since I returned to these shores. Winter dawns pink with crystal trimmings. Sky and sea are uniformly clad in corduroy stripes, the latter favouring a sheened rayon variety while sky's version is fleecy-lined.

With rimed snow on the ground and a nipsiccar wind that could cut barbed wire, I head for Windhouse on the hillside above Whalfirth. The place is said to be haunted and finding several half-eaten sheep-skulls on the track nearby, I am inclined to think the Hound of the Baskervilles may also be in residence. It is definitely a spooky looking place as you may judge for yourself…

> *But now I only hear*
> *It's melancholy, long, withdrawing roar,*
> *Retreating, to the breath*
> *Of the night-wind, down the vast edges drear*
> *And naked shingles of the world.*
> (Extract from Matthew Arnold Dove's *Dover Beach*)

SEA VIEW

Scalloway Castle. *(See page 2)*

SEA VIEW

Above: **Midwinter in Mid Yell.** A copper sea in the eerie light of dawn. This is not a sepia print; it is a true likeness of what confronts me as I wait for sun to colour my world.

Below: **Breckon Beach, Yell.** *(See page 21)*

SEA VIEW

Above: **A giant tooth on the cliffs of West Yell.** *(See page 8)*

Left: **"Sea Change" scarf.**
(See page 23/24)

Below: **The Yin and Yang of land and sea.**

SEA VIEW

Above: **Waiheke Beach, New Zealand.** *(See page 36)*

Below: **Hardy hill-sheep.**

SEA VIEW

Above: **A new angle on cormorants.** *(See page 26)*

Below: **Otter with lumpfish, Mid Yell.** *(See page 46)*

SEA VIEW

Christmas Eve on Bressay. *Photo by Charles Umphray. (See page 32)*

SEA VIEW

Where land lies sloped to the sea's rim and speckled with snow it is like a beached seal.

SEA VIEW

Picture window in a ruined Mid Yell building.

SEA VIEW

Incoming tide is hounding waves onto the beach. I sit timing the rhythm (about every five seconds) and contemplate how best to phonetically represent the sound. Hurrrrrussssss, sssskrunch, krrrrroooosh, grrrrraaaashhhhh. Very much like the echo of thunder grumbling behind distant clouds. Some other words come to mind. Affrug, brennastyooch, bretsh, fram, gremster, löragub, saatbrack, shoormal, shorebod, skudd, snaar. No, not Russian swear-words or the sound of someone throwing up; these are some of the many Shetland dialect words used to describe various appearances or actions of the sea. All have their origins in the old (Norn) language that was once the mother tongue of Shetland, and all are known and used to this day by dialect-speaking Shetlanders. It is further evidence of the way in which sea dominates people's lives in this place and the extent to which tradition (and indeed superstition) plays a major part when one speaks of the sea. There are close on 200 words related to the subject and upward of 100 more to do with the weather. For many years after English

SEA VIEW

began to be superimposed on the local language, fishermen (and especially deep-sea fishermen) retained the old words when they were offshore. In time the 'sea-words' came to be termed 'tabu' (taboo) although it was really the English, and to a lesser degree the Scots, words that were taboo.

Irrespective of how social and population changes might further impinge on and erode the Shetland dialect, old Norn words associated with sea and weather will indubitably be the last to go. If nothing else, they are so picturesquely descriptive. Brennastyooch! Now, that's much better than krrrrooooosh.

I am being ferried across Yell Sound in bright moonlight at 9pm. Now *there's* a different sea view! One worth going up to the passenger lounge for. Any light reflecting from the sea is likely to educe a positive response though moonlight has to be the most evocative. The *Wizard of Oz's* Yellow Brick Road, if you will, potentially hazardous to cross but leading to the Emerald City. Lead me on.

Wind sings a tight-stringed keening song; a song of bleak, desolate places. Sea knows this song also, carrying its meter in precisely modulated cadence until it fractures like crystal against rocky shores. Wind song is less easily quieted, spinning on a warped turntable of isobars with a needle stuck in its groove. All day I listen, half expecting a change of tune but it only increases in volume. And throughout the night it continues…

… until, in the morning, sky is "hanging on the ground", to use a local expression. In other words, there is little to distinguish one from the other. And while you are at it you can lump in sea to complete the picture. It is a monotone day. Wind has not abated. Outside the sheltered voe, sea will be doing battle with any and all-comers. (Forgive this correspondent if he doesn't actually travel to the war zone to confirm the news.)

On a better day and in bright sunshine I head to South Yell, aiming to walk back to the Horse of Burravoe (a prominent headland that turns out to look more like a sloth, but that's by-the-by). A strong south-easterly is blowing in off the sea fetching huge waves to come crashing all along the cliffs, further enhancing the spectacular scene. It is not particularly cold; certainly nothing like the past several days. At this time of year sunshine is afforded an all too brief window of opportunity – seldom more than a couple of hours. For once, I manage to make the most of what is on offer.

High on the moor I pass an Ordnance Survey trig-point. A good spot from which to obtain a panoramic view. Below me, the mossy slope falls steeply to the sea. In places the gradient is 45 degrees or more. Too steep for safe walking above the cliffs, yet sheep tracks traverse it at several levels. A flock of a hundred or more cormorants are standing on one of these steep patches of grass at the cliff's edge. I am able to approach from above without unduly alarming them and obtain several dramatic photographs. The strong on-shore wind whips up and over them. I think they must have their toes locked into the grass in order to hang on! *(See photo page v)*.

Deep steep-sided geos are a feature here, each having a waterfall in its apex where the sodden hinterland drains out. Approaching one, I am met with a

SEA VIEW

shower of spray that is being driven vertically up the cliff. What do you call a waterfall that is defying gravity?

Farther on, I crouch in a sheltered spot for a while, watching the sea crashing in the mouth of a cave. Backwash is churned to opaque aqua while further out the sea is navy blue. Against the cliffs is a cauldron of boiling foam. Updraft off the sea is carrying snowball-sized clumps of this foam straight up the cliffs and flinging them up to 200 yards inland where they cling to the heather like sprouted mushrooms. All around me is high drama. Shakespeare has its measure:

> *"The noontide sun called forth the mutinous winds,*
> *And twixt the green sea and the azured vault*
> *Set roaring war – "*
> (*The Tempest* Act 5, Scene 1: 40)

Returning to Burravoe pier, I pass four examples of houses that span the better part of as many centuries. The oldest is well down the slope close to the sea. An unroofed ruin snugly noosted in the hill; dry-stone walls skilfully erected to stand the test of time. It would originally have been thatched. Its conjoined byres still tell of economy and practicality in an unsophisticated age. A little higher up and perhaps built a hundred years later, the next house is likewise empty although not strictly a ruin. It still boasts a roof – this one made of tarred felt. Houses of this sort can be found all over Shetland. No longer habitable, they are referred to as 'vod hooses'. Many of these have been renovated over the past century, usually by raising the gables to accommodate low-ceilinged dormer windowed bedrooms on a second floor. Sometimes the tiny windows are enlarged to let in extra light and, of course, mod cons are added along with front and back porches. Higher up the slope is an example of one of these. Still lived in, it is neat and trig with whitewashed walls and a freshly tarred black roof. It may not have double-glazing or central heating but its thick walls and cavity ceiling will ensure it is snug enough. Smoke from a gable chimney indicates an open fire or slow-combustion stove. Possibly peat-burning, though not necessarily.

At the top of the hill, with by far the best view (and by far the worst exposure to the elements), stands a large two-storey detached dwelling that boasts everything our up-to-the-minute consumer society demands. Pseudo-tiled roof (and more than likely pseudo-wooden floors); aluminium window frames, Satellite television disc at a gable end. In all probability, the walls are built of some sort of prefabricated material. They have been rendered with rough-cast and painted in a trendy shade of puce. Of the four, this one is the least attractive. Totally unsuited to its environment, it stands out like a sore thumb. Like so many of its sort, it has built-in obsolescence. I give it 60-80 years.

I like the noosted one at the bottom of the hill best. Entirely unliveable from a human perspective it is still a home for others. Starlings nest in its wall cavities and will have done so for a couple of hundred years or more; sheep böl here in inclement weather and mice creep into its corners in search of wind-blown seeds.

SEA VIEW

Its worn steps and hearthstones keep memories of in-gatherings and tales told by an open fireside. There is all manner of history stacked up in these stones.

A peerie stream runs past my door – little better than a ditch really yet it babbles cheerily 24/7 (as they say). I hear it when I wake in the night and its light-hearted chuckling makes me smile. Rising who-knows-where in the hills behind the house and picking up gossip all along the way, it comes bursting with news and unable to keep a secret, spilling everything to the ponderous sea where such trifling snippets are treated with censorious contempt and promptly waved aside. Does that bother my happy little stream? Not a bit of it. It just goes right on babbling.

A long ribbon winds down the hill, round the end of the voe and out through the valley. It is bumper-to-bumper cars moving slowly from kirk to graveyard behind a hearse. At the graveyard, a crowd drifts together; a sea of black moving indecisively between headstones towards an open grave. In the loch nearby, whooper swans form into another drift of uncertainty, watching the incongruous congregation on the slope above them. Two flocks – one white, one black. And the grey sea further out, murmuring a measured response to the preacher's committal: earth to earth, ashes to ashes, dust to dust. Laid to rest in a place of exquisite beauty and peace while sea delivers its own eternal requiem. All life arose first from the sea's embryonic fluidity and all life is sustained by water, therefore "water to water" might be a better mantra.

On a brighter day, I make an early start under clear skies. For once I can utilise all that the sun has to offer and decide on approaching the Horse of Burravoe from the Gossabrough side. First things first. After parking the car, I enjoy a cup of coffee and a chat with David and Beatrice. From here, I head round the Ness of Gossabrough before turning south towards the Horse. Peter Guy (*Walking the Coastline of Shetland, No 1 The Island of Yell*; The Shetland Times Ltd, 1996) describes this region as "one of the main sea bird breeding areas in Shetland" and so this is very much about reconnoitring for future visits in spring and summer.

The Horse is a place of spectacular cliffs. One can walk the length of its back (500 yards or so) right out to the 'head' or Stack of the Horse. Although it is plenty wide for safe walking, I can't help thinking it is as well this horse doesn't buck! The cliffs, especially on the southern side, are awesome. After three days of calm weather, the sea is correspondingly subdued. This would be a fearsome place on a rough day. Natural arches (what's 'natural' about them I'd like to know?) are easily admired from the saddle and looking back to the Point of Whitehill the deep cleft known as Revri Geo is further evidence of sea's destructive forces. Returning to Gossabrough, I find David has been keeping a lookout for me and I am invited in for further refreshment. Shetland hospitality can be very persuasive and I am easily persuaded!

The next day is calm, clear and bright with frost lying like snow. All day the voe keeps its polished steel surface so that every passing boat leaves a signature. Watching the pleated ripples expand is like watching an old black and white television with faulty horizontal hold. By the time these shockwaves have

SEA VIEW

patterned the entire surface all the way to the shore, sea has the appearance of a Venetian blind that has been stretched out for cleaning. It is difficult to drag myself away from the hypnotic slow-motion animation being played out under clear skies.

I have a chart showing the daily changes in sunrise and sunset across the entire year for Lerwick. While I have been aware for most of my life that the longest night is between 20th and 21st December, I am intrigued to note the way in which rise and set times alter across the two or three weeks either side of these dates.

Sunrise today (12th December) is at 9am. By 26th December it will have reached its latest rise time of 9.10am, returning again to 9am by 10th January. This is a 10-minute difference across 30 days. Meanwhile, in the same period sunset goes from 2.57pm today to 2.56pm two days later and remains at this time for a total of five consecutive days, returning to 2.57pm on 20th and 21st (the shortest days). By 10th January it is setting at 3.25pm, making a 28-minute variation across the same 30 days. Doubtless there is a perfectly straightforward scientific reason why this discrepancy between sunrise and sunset times occurs; something to do with earth's axis perhaps.

We remain under the influence of a large area of high barometric pressure with correspondingly clear skies and calm sea. I return to West Sandwick in the hope of getting another look at the otter I saw there a few weeks ago. It is low tide and in the frosty, calm conditions it is difficult to approach the region without running the risk of being observed. Nevertheless, I am lucky. Two otters are feeding in shallow water amongst partially submerged patches of seaweed. At times it is difficult to distinguish them from the swirling kelp but gradually they come closer and my patience is rewarded when one climbs out on some rocks where it grooms itself for a few minutes. It is about forty or fifty yards from me and consequently at the outer extremity of my camera's telephoto capacity for such small objects. The photos are not particularly good, being of substantially reduced mega pixels. I am in no way disappointed however, knowing that many people come to Shetland in search of otters and have no luck at all. It is a real privilege to sit and watch these beautiful animals, knowing how vulnerable they are as man continues to exploit their habitats and compete with them for fish. This very day I hear on *BBC Scotland* and read in *The Shetland Times* that road-kill of otters in Shetland may be as high as 10 per cent of the total population annually.

Brough – broch – fort (Old Norse: *borg*). These circular dry-stone constructions date from around 1st century BC and are thought to have been built for defensive purposes, or as high status homes. Most sites in Shetland (Shetland Amenity Trust lists 115) are unidentifiable to the untrained eye, being little more than vaguely circular in shape and largely underground, robbed out or overgrown; notable exceptions being Mousa and Clickimin which are celebrated tourist attractions. Most appear to have been built for strategic purposes though whether for their impregnability or to draw attention to themselves by virtue of their deliberately

SEA VIEW

conspicuous locations still divides expert opinion. Either or both reasons seem to be distinct possibilities as the choice of sites varies enormously.

Brochs are believed to be peculiar to Scotland and are associated with the enigmatic Picts. The majority are situated in the Western Isles, north Scottish coastal region, and Orkney and Shetland. Shetland is thought to have the highest concentration. Many have remained virtually undisturbed for centuries owing to their remoteness.

During my coastal walks I make a point of seeking out as many brochs as possible (almost all are on the coast) and have marvelled at the ingenuity and single-mindedness of the architects who frequently chose sites that must have posed considerable problems for the builders. One such site is on a headland or 'ness' aptly named The Brough, near West Sandwick in Yell. This narrow, steep-sided site is cut off at high tide although admittedly this would not necessarily have been the case when the broch was built around 2000 years ago. There is evidence of ramparts below the main structure which dominates the spot. All but a few stones have now sunk below earth's surface leaving a large circular hollow with very little space between it and the cliffs on all sides. While there is no shortage of building material in the surrounding area, getting the rocks up the cliff face would have been a mammoth task requiring both skill and brute strength. In its day, this broch must have dominated the coast and would have been immediately apparent to any ship entering Yell Sound from either north or south. If this was a high-status dwelling then its owners chose well. It is a strikingly beautiful place and such prominence could not fail to impress. As a fort, it would have been well-nigh impregnable.

While it is tempting to conjecture what might be gained by archaeological investigation of the West Sandwich broch, there can be little doubt that it would pose a logistical nightmare for anyone so engaged. However, another millennium of pounding seas (especially one adversely affected by climate change) will, in all likelihood, destroy the site forever.

My friend Steven, who lives beside a different warmer sea, takes delight in reminding me of it. He is on Waiheke Island in the Hauraki Gulf near Auckland, New Zealand, and sends regular emails in which he likes to refer to the "… hot nights and long sunny days". He writes of "… fine days with a gentle breeze, the Gulf so blue and happy that you'd swear you were looking into the eyes of an angel". Knowing that I am searching for suitable words to describe cold briny, Steven rubs in salt with taunting phrases like "balmy breezes in my Hauraki paradise". My problem lies in that I have been there and I know he is right!

But even in a semi-tropical paradise, sea and sky may turn morbid. On another day Steven sends me this:

"… sad slipping sheets of grey-and-white and Ramses's own darkness has descended unto us. Towards Oneroa the world has disappeared into a veil of grey… … loud, dripping, thundering, vengeful… grey Gulf dusted with regret… crying greens hunkering under heavy hollow hues… desolate breezes blowing over utter greyness in humid headiness…".

SEA VIEW

Not particularly conducive to my packing a bag and flying over there! Yet it is only marginally better here. The sea is 'choppy'. My dictionary defines the word as meaning: "rough sea on which the surface of the water is broken up into many small waves caused by strong winds". But by evening the word on everyone's lips is "snow". Now, there's something to sleep on…

… or wake to! Except I don't. London? Yes, heavy snowfall and all the usual associated disruptions to public transport. Not here, however. We are smug (I'd be lying if I said snug) under a blanket of cloud and the sea is passive – not even choppy! Our day will come…

Contemplating the season's foreshortened days can lead to dark thoughts. Sea can scarcely turn a tide before day's curtain-call has been curtailed and night has stolen a march, half its lines and all the stage. It really is too bad. Or is it? Surely the darkest night permits some light – or its reflection darkly revealed – for sea is never so black-hearted that it does not return a fallen star or allow phosphorescence its tiny moment of glory. And no wave breaks without showing its teeth.

In the midst of a blizzard, sea is the darkest feature. There is no skyline. (What Shetlanders call "a blinndin moorie caavie".) Slowly the landscape becomes whiter until all is blanketed. And still it falls; rounding out the hollows, blunting sharp edges, plastering every vertical surface and levelling the playing field in some misbegotten notion of political correctness – under EU regulations if it's snowing in Brussels then it ought to be snowing here. Only sea stoically maintains its independence, sternly frowning in gunmetal grey. And yet it is sorely pressed, making a token concession by wearing an ermine hem; the reverse image of a black arm-band worn in mourning.

Le Roi est mort. Vive le Roi! The storm is dead. Long live the storm! (Not a translation, but you get my drift; as the snowstorm said to the wall.) We are in the eerie calm of the eye and nervously awaiting the next blast. The last came out of Iceland; the next will come from Siberia – or Outer Mongolia! It will indeed be "snow on snow".

My friend in New Zealand describes his scene on midsummer's day as "grey gloom incarnate". It is the very same here (except it is midwinter). The sky's dome is like the inside of a pot – unblemished dull pewter. An old beer tankard. The ground is still white but no longer pristine as a thaw is under way. It has become rather grubby. In contrast, my sea is strangely luminous. It matches the sky except that someone has taken a polishing cloth to it and made it shine like antique silver. All a bit surreal, with a funereal hush hanging over everything. I am expecting pall-bearers to come round the corner any minute. Their breath will freeze in the air and their footsteps will be muffled by the snow. Soon the church bell will begin tolling and I will watch fearfully to discover on which chimney-pot a black crow will alight – for it is to there the pall-bearers will go…

Words! How easily we twist them. Enough! 'tis the season to be jolly! I shall climb to the top of the highest hill and tear away this grey curtain of morbidity. Somewhere above it there is a star.

*A man by the name of Davy Moar who lived at Sellafirth, on Basta Voe, owned a tievin (thieving) moorit (brown) yowe that kept breaking in to all the gardens in the neighbourhood, eating vegetables and flowers and generally making a mess of things. Davy decided to banish the animal to the island of Hascosay, which lies across the mouth of Basta Voe. No one lives on Hascosay so it was reckoned the sheep would cause no further problems. However, for a bit of fun, some of the lads rowed out and fetched the ewe back, releasing it in the field below Davy's house. Next morning it was back in its owner's garden and Davy presumed it must have swum home. A homing sheep! Impossible as this had to be, the word got around and the delinquent animal swiftly attained fame throughout Yell and beyond, becoming known as "the moorit yowe o' Hascosay" which in turn led to the saying "as **weel kent** as the moorit yowe o' Hascosay".*

At this time of year, and at this latitude, daylight is at a premium and people tend to become preoccupied with created light of any kind. ("It is better to light just one little candle than to stumble in the dark…") Some will attend Watch Night services to herald Christmas Day, dwelling on the coming 'Light of the World', others will trim their trees with fairy lights, deck the halls and generally burn the candle at both ends.

Two ferries take us through calm seas and exquisite light effects to where we will spend Christmas and Boxing Day. I am so entranced by the play of light in sea and sky that I can scarcely take it in. All about me are precious jewels, pools of gold, hills of sparkling diamonds and platinum seas. Surely there can be no more beautiful spot on earth than the one on which I am standing. In the event it is Charlie who takes the better picture *(see photo page vi)*.

After Christmas dinner I go for a short walk along the shore. Some seals are lying on a bed of seaweed-covered rock taking an afternoon nap. They too appear to have over-eaten and I get the distinct impression that my company is not welcome. I can take a hint. Besides, the idea of an afternoon nap has suddenly become very inviting and I'm not thinking of a bed of seaweed!

Today I take a longer walk, all of it by way of a reflective sea view. I negotiate a slippery breakwater; pass a mirrored marina; travel round a narrow voe into which sky has fallen in dazzling beauty to match the view of Christmas Eve; traverse a grassy ness where seabirds are huddled in clumps of long grass trying to keep warm; and finally come to where the Bressay ferry *Leirna* is lying behind her breakwater. Beyond lies the narrow channel across which I can hear the half-hour being chimed on Lerwick's Town Hall clock. Freezing air and frozen ground have subdued all life or at least brought it to a temporary standstill. Yesterday's seals are still sleeping it off and behind tinselled windows I suspect the island's population is doing likewise. Only one other person ventures forth, passing by with hands in pockets and giving me an "aye, aye" to my "fine day" greeting.

There was a time when Boxing Day brought tradesmen to your door seeking their 'box' or handout for services rendered throughout the year. A sort of

SEA VIEW

belated VAT. They should be so lucky – or we should. It is all 'flat packs' and DIY these days. Tradesmen? Now there's a novel idea.

Scientists contend that the phenomenon known to surfers as "the seventh wave" is a myth. Surfers claim to know otherwise, and will count waves in the firm belief that to catch the seventh in a set will guarantee them the ultimate ride. Even beach bums will tell you there is rhyme and reason in the waves. And who amongst us has not, at some time or other, become preoccupied with wave counting, if only to keep from getting our feet wet as we zigzag along that playfully unpredictable curl of foam as it hisses in over the sand. Returning to the island of Yell today, counting seventh waves is not an option owing to choppy seas and tidal roosts. It would be easier to count chickens before they hatch.

> *The north wind will blow and there will be snow,*
> *And what will poor Robin do then, poor thing?*
> *He'll sit in a barn to keep himself warm,*
> *And hide his head under his wing.*

Ten days in this deep freeze and the novelty is definitely wearing off. Putting one foot in front of the other is a hazardous undertaking. Silken sea and satin sky are both wearing hat-lining shades of grey. And now the Arctic wind blows colder to deliver flurries of fresh snow. By way of contrast, I learn of a family member in Australia buying DVDs for Christmas and putting them in an ice-box to keep them from warping (or melting!). The interior temperature of the car was 47 degrees! Right now I'd settle for the seven.

You will be familiar with those packets of gourmet smoked salmon found on supermarket shelves. That is the texture and colour of this morning's sea. Sun has risen out of clear skies in the southern quarter while to the north high cumulus is a frivolous froth of… you guessed it, salmon – except the clouds are a creamier version of sea's sliced variety. All of it will have a short shelf-life and we may surmise that those clouds are the harbinger of something distinctly less frivolous. Meanwhile, in calm air, I intend to enjoy the spectacular beauty of it all.

And I am not alone…

My email inbox has this message sent from Tasmania:

"Hey dad, writing this email on my mobile phone, it's close to midnight and I have just cleaned up camp and wandered down to the shore of Macquarie Harbour inland from Hells Gates. Its day 5 of a ten day 4wd safari tour with an American family and with the long summer days my working days are usually from 5am till 11pm! It's close to a full moon and dead calm, with clear starry skies above, very unusual for the west coast. Anyway it's frustratingly hard to write on a phone.

"Have a happy New Year, Ben."

"… close to a full moon and dead calm, with clear starry skies…"
Snap! … if you allow for poles apart in temperature.

This is the twelfth consecutive day on which some snow has fallen. Partial thaws between times have made for messy (and dangerous) road conditions. Being unable to go out and about much I am beginning to get an inkling of what Alaskans mean when they talk of 'cabin fever'. Of course, they are referring to a time when there was no television and they were restricted to re-reading Jack London or Robert Service for the umpteenth time. Come to think of it, I'd happily swap the current offerings on TV for either of the above.

All this preoccupation with weather inevitably turns one's thoughts to global warming. The latest predictions have many of the world's coastal regions being inundated by up to one metre before the end of the century. This would result in catastrophic loss of land and buildings. *National Geographic* explains that this scenario will be caused not only by melting icecaps but by a process known as 'thermal expansion' (warmer water takes up more room than colder water). And, in case anyone thinks the debate is just so much hot air, try this particular statistic for size: "The complete melting of Greenland would raise sea levels by seven metres (23 feet)" (*National Geographic*). It seems everyone's sea view may be about to change.

Be that as it may, tonight the sea is a sounding board. Across the water at North-a-Voe a number of residents have established a Hogmanay custom of visiting *all* the houses in the district, finishing at the eastern extremity of their village. Carrying flaming torches, they proceed in a long line back through the village to the opposite end where they light a bonfire on the beach and have a party. The sea's sounding board comes into play in that the torchlight procession blow horns and trumpets to attract the attention of their neighbours (that's us) across the voe. Hearing the noise we are alerted to a festive spectacle which on a calm night like tonight is reflected on the water.

Happy New Year!

"Goin' roond the hooses" is what Hogmanay is all about in this neck of the woods. Some would add "until the hooses are goin' roond you". We make it home at 2.30am and we are amongst the early ones! If you don't turn out your lights you may expect to continue receiving visitors until daylight. Walking home by moonlight along the seafront in those 'wee sma' oors' I am wondering what the New Year has in store for me and where these reflective fragments will take me in the coming months.

Take an oar, boy! Out beyond yon baa is where the fish are and you have no more right to them than the least of us, unless you pull your weight. Look at Charlie, bending his back and breaking sweat upon his brow. Match him (if you can) or I foresee us going in circles for the rest of the day.

That's more like it.

No need to overdo it though. See! You'll have us in the roost. Rest on your oar a moment and look how the water churns. We'll give that one a wide berth if it's all the same to you. I've no desire to be carried a mile out to sea, let alone be put upon the reef.

SEA VIEW

Now steady as she goes.

I'm telling you, there's fish in that piece of black water... there, where I'm pointing. And I suppose it would be asking too much of you all to coordinate your efforts a little so as to stop this confounded dithering back and forth. One would think you were skiing down the Matterhorn to look at you...

And on and on he went; his hand on the tiller (though he never bothered to move it) and a pipe in the corner of his mouth. If he'd not been such an old man and therefore due a little respect, they might have...

No, perish the thought.

> *Overhead the sky was full of strings and shreds of vapour, flying, vanishing, reappearing, and turning about an axis like tumblers, as the wind hounded them through heaven.*
> *Travels with a Donkey* (R.L. Stevenson)

How like today's scene in which skeins of rain are making sea where the sky ought to be and all the clouds have tumbled down to drown in the ocean. Between times flurries of snow drive horizontally through middle earth unwilling to be tagged with any of the elements. They are akin to flocks of shorn sheep relentlessly pursued and badgered by invisible packs of dogs until driven far south, rounded up in steep corries beyond Ben Nevis or chivvied into the Yorkshire Dales to be buried under more of the same, sifted and drifted, walled in then frozen out.

Today's sea has the rare beauty and increased refractive properties of hand cut lead crystal. Its multi-faceted surface gleams with an inner beauty that is more than skin-deep. Even the glistening snow must defer to this adamantine splendour. At sunset sky competes with land and sea till every element is imbued with the same fiery drama that inspired Turner's Venetian masterpieces.

Now on the twentieth consecutive day on which some snow has fallen, Shetland schools have not yet reopened since the Christmas break owing to extremely hazardous road conditions. Yet the depth of snow here is inconsequential when compared with other parts of UK where many counties are experiencing their worst winter in thirty years. Temperatures have fallen to minus 20 degrees Celsius in some parts, airports have been closed and public transport has come to a standstill. And the sea? It is calmly serene. All the brouhaha surrounding the icy conditions has scarcely caused a ripple. The sea's rim is rimed. There is a cryogenic crust that delineates the high tide mark. Below it is a narrow ice-free corridor along which one can walk without fear of falling. To attempt walking anywhere else is a hazardous undertaking.

At low tide the exposed sand known as 'the links' which is directly below our house, has become a popular spot for all manner of birdlife. The ebb-feeders come in search of food while others simply congregate to stand and stare. It is as if they derive reassurance from the familiarity of the terrain and the sea view when all else has turned alien.

If there are degrees of calm then today must be the nth. Being a Sunday morning and still early, nothing is stirring. Sky is a cloudless arc of the palest ice blue. Sea is mother-of-pearl. All else remains crystallized in frozen fields of snow. On the skyline at the far side of the village, the glass shield of a street lamp has caught the sun. It is a shining star; a gleaming diamond in today's tiara.

And at day's end I have six miles of memorable coast walking and some special photos to keep this date alive in my mind. In a lifetime underscored by beautiful days there have been few that have been more captivating. Returning home in the last glimmer of light, I am treated to exquisite shades of mauve, aquamarine, lilac, pale rose, lime, lark's egg blue, lemon… and that's just the sky! Nor will sea be outdone; stealing all of sky's colours and tingeing them with deeper hues (jade, viridian, cobalt) then adding ice to mix a psychedelic cocktail that would knock your socks off. Here's to today… Skoal!

A night to take in the piltock wand. In conversation, an acquaintance recalls this saying from early last century. It refers to taking indoors the long fishing rod (used for catching piltocks) when extremely heavy snow has been forecast. The old croft houses were low, single storey buildings tucked into the sides of the hills. In severe blizzards they might be reconciled to becoming buried under snow. In the event of this occurring the cane pole could be thrust up the chimney with a piece of bright cloth attached to it so that rescuers might find the house and dig it out. In this particular fall of snow the covering in Shetland is only a few inches deep, however it is entirely possible that some old cottages in the Scottish highlands could be so threatened as to benefit from this kind of insurance.

But now the thaw is on in earnest. My little stream had stopped running, frozen in its mossy genesis high in the hills behind the house or hung in suspense along steep banks – crystal chandeliers winking at the sun. Only today, when I hear it again, does it come to me that my recent yesterdays have been silent and I was unwittingly deprived of a favourite song.

And what of the sea; did it sough in contentment to be quit of incessant chatter or did it creep in across the sand grudgingly acknowledging the loss of that fresh taste in its salty mouth?

The Beaches of Waiheke

On our migratory route home to Shetland from Tasmania, we stopped off to winter on Waiheke Island in the Hauraki Gulf near Auckland, New Zealand.

The island has a population of around 8000, many of whom commute to work in Auckland, 12 miles across the water. In summer, the population increases to over 30,000 when holidaymakers head out to crowd the beaches or moor their yachts in one or other of the sheltered bays. Our time on the island coincided with the 'off-season', nevertheless there were still plenty of boats about – houseboats on the tidal mud-flats, colourful dinghies stacked end-on above the beaches, and pleasure craft moored in every bay.

The island is hilly and much of it is covered in semi-tropical vegetation. On every side, leafy paths zigzag down to the beaches from the steep slopes. Features of the terrain are the Pohutukawa trees, which grow all over the island, their twisted trunks and branches reaching out across the sand at the tide's edge to form shade umbrellas from the hot sun. In summer, these trees produce bright red flowers, making a striking picture against the white sand. And in the midst of this arctic-like winter, what better way to pass the time than in conjuring up the beaches of Waiheke in my mind's eye? *(See photo page iv).*

A day of different weather, which in turn prompts this rose spectacled quote: "Sunshine is delicious, rain is refreshing, wind braces us up, snow is exhilarating; there is no such thing as bad weather, only different kinds of good weather."

(John Ruskin 1819-1900)

Hmm… well, I note Ruskin wrote that little piece of philosophy before global warming became an issue. He might like to rephrase it in the current climate because what I am looking at today is not a 'different kind of good weather'. It is filthy weather in the making. With snow virtually all gone and wind rising, sea is back in contention having played a passive role for the last few weeks. No longer the reflective onlooker, it is in assertive mood. A hungry beast of prey with its tail lashing.

The thump of waves breaking and the cry of gulls, these are the quintessential sounds of Shetland that only impact on the subconscious after we have been deprived of them for several days, as when a prolonged calm lays a hush over everything. But it is the gulls that I am particularly aware of now. Were they truly silent during those days of eerie stillness or was that my imagination? Did I simply block out their cries, not wishing anything to break the spell, or were they similarly influenced and struck dumb?

And by nightfall the beach is being pounded as wind increases and sea responds. With my incessantly prattling streamlet on one side and the sonorous measured pulsation of churning surf on the other, I am being serenaded by nature's own sleep-inducing contrapuntal symphony.

> *A life on the ocean wave,*
> *A home on the rolling deep,*
> *Where the scattered waters rave,*
> *And the winds their revels keep.*
>
> Epes Sargent

Little boats are braving the elements with prows plunging through heavy swell to send shivering spray over the thwarts. Some life! Some home! I have unqualified admiration for all men who go to sea in fishing boats of whatever sort. In these waters it is a bone-chilling thankless task.

Blow the wind southerly, southerly, southerly… I recall this song from my school days. It was always sung to a slow, plodding, metronomic beat that totally contradicted the south wind as we knew it. And today's southerly is a howling gale fit to pluck any metronome from the shelf and send it flying to the North Pole. Add a flood tide to the equation and you may know sea is making serious inroads up and down the coast. Force 10 (so they say) with a sky full of tattered clouds scudding northwards and rain flissing like wet sheets on a line or a saturated shaggy dog bounding along a beach.

In the entrance to Mid Yell voe is a tiny islet called Kay Holm. At the south end of the holm is a sunburst shape of what looks to be ditches that run from the plateau on the top down to the sea. No one has lived or worked on Kay Holm in living memory and no one can shed any light on why such ditches might have been dug; yet they are clearly defined, even showing up on the satellite images of Google Maps. What is more, they appear to have been precisely engineered.

Such a minute space on top of so insignificant a little islet could scarcely warrant drainage ditches of this elaborate magnitude. Might I read into these deliberately etched lines some ancient symbolism associated with pagan worship? Did druid priests enact gory blood sacrifices within these meids while solemn-faced tribesmen looked down from the top of nearby Hevdagarth? Or is this a landing pad for extra-terrestrials?

Ian shows me his gallery of otter photographs. Most have been taken within half a mile of his home at Burravoe, South Yell. The images are stunning and many are worthy of being published in wildlife magazines. I am envious of his

Kay Holm, featuring the "crop marks".

camera, his talent, and his obvious patience, as such photographs require all three.   In conversation, I learn that Burravoe is one of the best places in Shetland for viewing otters. Clearly, I am going to have to spend more time in the locality if I want to enjoy their company, and if Ian's photos are anything to go by, otters are the most engaging of wildlife company.

Another flying gale, with spume blowing off wave-tops and surf crashing over sea walls to create mayhem in marinas. Salt spray is streaking across every polished surface and down every window pane, leaving them bleared and smeared while rust (its partner in crime) viciously attacks the underside of my car like a hungry rodent in a granary. I'm being got at. When I leave the house, wind is waiting around the corner to ambush me, flinging knifes honed on ice then snatching my cap before buffeting me mercilessly; all the while screaming obscenities and taunts to wear down my resistance before threatening to wrench the car door off its hinges when I cautiously open it. A little way up the road, I see children running outside the school with their coats turned inside-out above their heads. It is a game I well remember from my own childhood. A laughing game in which wind always has the last laugh, sending its challengers tumbling head-over-heels like tossed leaves.

Now in the allotted span of years with youth's resilience gone, I must wrap my coat tight about me, bow to the wind and breathlessly beg its mercy. But whatever the outcome I know I can still chance the wind. Sea on the other hand makes no concessions, brooks no shirkers and takes no prisoners. It wears a gossamer gown today; one that folds and flows under a wind-shredded sky. Brief glimpses of sunshine float ethereally in vertical beams. If I strike one with a hammer it might shatter or ring out in fine humour like a bell. A beached wave is trying to hush chattering pebbles at the sea's rim. It has as much chance as King Canute who recognised the futility of attempting to turn the tide. "Let all men know how empty and worthless is the power of kings," he said. "There is none worthy of the name except He whom the heavens and earth and sea obey by eternal laws". But they did not listen.

There is a dead gull in the ebb. I saw it yesterday, before it died. An old, blind bird come to its last; its feathers broken and tattered; its head hung low. Jonathon Livingston? I think not. This once sleek wanderer; this wave-top drifter that has limped home on a wing and a prayer to die: sea will bleach its bones when scavengers have picked them clean and feathers will be recycled to line another's nest. Nature's waste-not-want-not lesson to slow learners.

> *Full fathom five thy father lies;*
> *Of his bones are coral made;*
> *Those are pearls that were his eyes:*
> *Nothing of him that doth fade*
> *But doth suffer a sea-change*
> *Into something rich and strange.*
>   William Shakespeare, 'The Tempest', Act 1 scene 2

A short hike in freezing conditions. The drip at the end of my nose is threatening to become an icicle. Ian and I bolster our spirits by imagining the loch at Vatsetter on a summer's day and us with fishing rods. Ian points out a picnic table on the strand between sea and loch. If we were to stop and sit here, we would in all probability become snap-frozen to the benches. Two ice-men subsequently turned to stone and become new-age monoliths for tourists to gawk at.

Up-Helly-A'

It is Shetland's fire festival to mark the end of the Yule season; once celebrated in 'tar-barrelling' – rolling barrels of burning tar through the streets – and now a pseudo-Viking affair involving guizers, a torchlight procession and the burning of a replica Viking galley. Does it have any historical significance? No. Does that bother anyone? No. Everyone simply pretends the practice has been going on for millennia when in fact it is less than 150 years since the first elements were introduced, and not until around the turn of last century that it began to take on the form of the modern-day event.

Always held on the last Tuesday of January, perhaps the most intriguing aspect of the whole affair is that despite all the shenanigans, the festival does *not* apparently warrant a public holiday. A holiday is declared for the day *after* – presumably in order to recover from the all-night revelry and the hang-over from hell that overtakes half the population.

Etymologists are undecided on the precise meaning of Up-Helly-A' although the dispassionate observer may note that the individual components of the word are frequently heard in the form of garrulous oaths or anguished groans along darkened streets in the wee small hours of Wednesday morning. With the passage of time, there is a distinct possibility that more A's will be added. Up-Helly-A-a-a-a-arrgh!

Last night's storm was of a sort to create problems for the festival's torchlight procession and send revellers scurrying for cover. Force 10 gusting to 11. A wild night by all accounts and definitely Up-Helly-A-a-a-arrgh!

Such storms bring compensation however. Sea-wrack! The urge to go beach-combing is in every Shetlander's genes. Ask any old man with a tell-tale stoop to his back to turn out his jeans' pockets and, as sure as God made little green apples, you'll be presented with some curio or other he has picked up off the beach. In the early hours of morning after a storm, you will see those dedicated men-of-the-seashore striding out towards their favourite beach or driving across the island to access a more likely spot – depending on the wind's direction. Anything found on or below the high-tidemark is reckoned 'finders-keepers'. Objects laid higher up the bank in orderly piles become private property of the original finder.

In a treeless environment, the most valued jetsam is wood. Planks, spars, boxes, even sticks and twigs are highly collectable. Whole trees, perhaps toppled by landslip or an avalanche across the North Sea in Norway and swept into the

SEA VIEW

sea, might end up on a Shetland beach, stripped of limbs, bark and foliage. Such treasure will probably require a tractor to complete the salvage. More commonly the finds will be related to merchant shipping or inshore fishing boats; things swept off a deck or accidentally dropped overboard – rope, creels, buoys, fish-boxes and the like. Then there are the little things, curios of every sort that come bobbing or rolling in on the tide. Strange, unidentified objects from around the globe that are destined to become bizarre decorations atop garden walls or ornaments in glass-fronted cabinets along with the china dogs and grandmother's favourite tea-set. And of course there is always the chance (however remote) of a bigger prize. A barrel of single malt whisky for instance. Or (fantasy in overdrive) doubloons! The hold of a Spanish galleon burst asunder on the seabed after hundreds of years, its treasure released to the tide.

I might have taken a turn along the beach myself this morning except that the weather has not let up. It will need to improve considerably before I'll be lured out. Doubtless, hardier types are not deterred and will get their rewards. They will be hard-earned in these conditions.

All day long the storm persists. Wind gradually turns more northerly exposing my patch of sea to ever-wilder waves. Squalls of freezing rain hurling down the voe are obliterating the landscape and battering against every vertical surface. Have all the hounds of hell been let loose?

A little boat is going about its workaday business amongst the mussel beds. For the crew it will be an extremely unpleasant task. Frozen hands. Lashing spray. Hazardous conditions. How could one not admire these men? Coward that I am, I keep to my couch all day.

I wake to a howling blizzard and the ground covered with snow. Drawing back the curtains, I'm met with the view of an otter walking across the open field about 70 yards away. It is carrying a live, struggling rabbit. Stopping beside a clump of grass (presumably for its meagre camouflage or protection from the wind) the sleek hunter settles to his breakfast. With flurries of snow blowing horizontally across the landscape it is impossible to obtain a photo of any quality but nevertheless I am rewarded with a grandstand view of this normally elusive mammal.

Decline of the otter population has been linked, in part, to over fishing of sandeels. If rabbit is now on the menu this may no longer be a problem as there is an abundance of rabbits in Shetland and they are easy prey for otters that can go down the burrows after them or pounce on them as they shelter under overhanging banks above the seashore.

Air temperature was -2° last night, which, with strong wind gusting up to 40mph, equates to a chill-factor of around -30°. I am thinking of that otter.

In the absence of body fat such as seals have, otters must rely on their fur alone to keep warm. They also need access to fresh water in order to clean out the salt after hunting in the sea else their fur would be damaged and lose much of its insulating qualities. Considering that they eat 15-20 per cent of their body weight daily in order to survive, and that fish is their main diet, it is not hard to

SEA VIEW

imagine the struggle they must have under these adverse conditions. If I was an otter I think I'd be honing my rabbit-hunting skills.

Meanwhile, the sea slowly gets colder; in fact, if it wasn't for the North Atlantic Drift we might expect it to freeze. It *looks* freezing. If an iceberg loomed up at the voe's entrance I wouldn't turn a hair. With otters still on my mind it comes as no surprise to see my visitor of two days ago purposefully retracing his steps. Overnight it has snowed some more and so he makes a fine spectacle undulating across the virgin surface like an over-eager puppy trying to insinuate his way into my affections – which he emphatically does. Now and again he pauses to roll in the snow before flowing on, nose to the ground and waggling bum in the air; comical and enchanting at one and the same time. A big fellow. Well over a metre in length I'd say, with weight of maturity in his girth. When he has passed from sight, I go out and photograph his trail. The five-toed paw marks are as big as a dog's while the tail's impression is clearly indented. We'll meet again. I'm sure of it. At 4pm, in fading light and on the back of yet another blizzard, I'm newly returned from the shop with smoked haddock for tea when I glance out the window to see the otter back-tracking his own trail. Passing the house, he deviates a little closer than on his outward journey this morning, giving me an even better view. His gait is more purposeful now as he heads down across the links to the sea. Clearly, he too has a fish supper in mind. I wish him luck.

There is a hike tent pitched in long grass beside a shed just above the beach. Can there really be someone in there? Yes. He emerges after sun-up at about 9.30, casually packs his gear in a rucksack and tramps away up the road. Experience has taught me that it can be remarkably warm inside a hike-tent; nevertheless, camping in such an exposed spot in these conditions appears to be a trifle masochistic.

Going for a walk in this weather involves putting on layers of protective clothing – hat, scarf, gloves, coat and boots, by which time you are like Michelin Man and hardly able to move. I dispense with a scarf by pulling my hat down over my ears and zipping my jacket right to the top. Hands in pockets mean I can do without gloves but that is all I can discard. The chill-factor (mentioned a couple of days ago) is no joke. But staying indoors on such a beautiful day is not to be contemplated, icy wind notwithstanding, and I set forth in high spirits crunching frozen snow under foot. I follow the coast for about a mile, still with otters uppermost in my mind. No luck. They are all snug in their holts. Sea is tarnished pewter that has thumbprints here and there on lightly buffed sections. One patch gleams like the interior of an oyster shell. Someone has made a proper job of polishing their bit.

Another wild night. Wind is working itself into a frenzy. Given that there are no trees or telephone lines for it to howl through, it is a wonder it manages to make such a fiendish noise.

More snow and a burnished copper-tinted sea (yesterday's tardy cleaners have turned over a new leaf). With sun taking station in blue sky, I'm planning a photographic foray… planning but not executing. In the time it takes to tap out these few words a battalion of clouds comes storming out of the north and lays siege to all. Sea blanches, sun ducks for cover and the world puts up its white flag of surrender. It is snowing again! But all is not lost. Out of the blue a truce is declared. Clouds march off in high dudgeon. Sun makes a comeback and sea puts on its smiley face. Now where did I leave the camera?

After a few more flurries of snow, we enter upon an afternoon of the sort that no amount of superlatives can hope to describe. Day's last movement is adagio. I watch it gently depart.

A porridge-for-breakfast day. Come to think of it, the landscape beyond my window is not dissimilar to the plate of porridge in front of me, except that it is colder, duller and decidedly lacking in taste. The entire sky resembles the inside of an egg, and I the embryo chicken eager to peck my way out. Freshening wind is stippling the sea making it the only animated feature in an otherwise freeze-framed scene.

A reflective view into yesterday afternoon's calm beauty.

SEA VIEW

Now the thaw is on in earnest. It is the price we have to pay for the beauty of snow. Every erg of earth's energy seems to be directed to the task, sucking any last semblance of heat out of the air to leave us all feeling robbed, naked and shivering. Roads are rivers of slush. Rivers are torrents. Hills weep. And the sea? It has turned strangely green and luminescent, as if lit from within. By tomorrow it will all have changed. The sheep will have grass again (we've been feeding the poor creatures over the fence with our potato peelings). Tomorrow, too, in corners of our garden where the snow has lain deep for weeks on end, there will be fat spring bulbs thrusting up to the light. For this I know: all life in Shetland, both below and above the ground, is eager for the return of light – so eager that the transformation it will bestow over the coming months will be nothing short of miraculous. It has to be seen to be believed. Spring in Shetland is sheer joy. But I am jumping the gun. Winter always keeps something up its sleeve. We are not done with it yet. It will doubtless have the last laugh.

"We are all in the same boat". How often this expression is used – in many cases by people who have never even seen the sea. It is an apt phrase nonetheless, especially in this age of globalisation. And if we *are* all in the same boat then it is the sea that will determine where we end our voyage for it becomes increasingly apparent that we have lost the rudder. Does this mean we are "all at sea"?

Winter's first snow of any consequence fell on 19th December and since then the ground has never been totally clear of it. Even after four days of thaw, it still lies in ditches and peat banks giving the landscape a mottled effect akin to the pelt of a snow leopard. Now temperature is again falling and the sky is full of snowy portents. Turn up the heat. Batten down the hatches. Here we go again… on second thoughts, maybe not… not yet, anyway.

I am walking the headland at Vatsetter to fill in a section of coastline I have missed. It is a bright day with a freshening northerly that has ice in its teeth. Along the low cliffs fulmars are skimming and diving past me like hurricanes, their gun-turret heads turning to rake me fore and aft in quizzical appraisal. There is poetry in the flight of these graceful birds and I never tire of watching them.

A long peat bank has been opened in the springy turf at the sea's edge. It is about four feet deep. A black wound being healed by sphagnum moss. It is good quality peat, cut as recently as last summer and some of it still lying in bags waiting to be taken home. It is not difficult to surmise its ultimate destination. I can smell the aromatic reek being blown from the chimney of a nearby croft house. Someone is sensibly saving on their power bill. Having peat at this proximity to one's house is like possessing your own coal mine. Better still, peat is easier to obtain, cleaner and lighter to handle. It smells nicer too.

Sea is chuckling amongst the rocks, retelling north wind's howler heard yesterday. The sombre-faced rocks do not appear about to split their sides though they have cracked a time or two when the joke has been on them in the past. More frequently, sea's sagas have been tumultuous and heartrending. Cliffs have caved in on hearing them. The entire coastline is an open book on an unfinished tale that is both funny and tragic; by part soothing, disturbing, epic, awesome and seemingly endless. From the beginning of time, all stories have begun in the sea. It will assuredly have the last say and the last laugh.

By nightfall our landlocked voe is becalmed. Sunset's afterglow is pure gold. There is frost in the air.

On a day of bright sunshine, I walk a favourite path out to the Brough at West Sandwick. Across Yell Sound, the upper slopes of Ronas Hill are still snow-covered. All else is green and brown with shining blue sea between. Tide is on the ebb exposing dulse that wafts tangy ozone. Overhead a noisy honking and gabbling causes me to raise my eyes. Over fifty greylag geese are strung out across the sky, heading north in a ravelled skein. Earth's pulse has quickened. There are good vibes here. *(See photo page ix)*.

Pax mare – peaceful sea. Not a breath of wind. There is a big and beautiful piece of sky in Vatsetter Loch and afternoon's stillness has laid a quieting hand on everything… well, almost everything. A mile away on the hillside at the far side of the loch a man is training a young sheep dog with the help of an older one. The shouted commands can be heard the length and breadth of the valley, causing sheep to bunch up in little knots of nervousness on every side. Presently the shepherd recalls his dogs and they jump into the back of his van. A few moments later, they arrive at the ayre where I am standing between sea and loch. We exchange greetings then the man releases his dogs for a romp in the sea. As they walk across close-cropped grass to the shore, I am touched by the young dog's devotion, his boundless enthusiasm and desire to ingratiate himself. Prancing like a pony, his eyes sparkling and his pink tongue lolling out the side of his mouth, he is eager to impress and please his master. Every couple of steps he takes are followed by a little gyrating dance as he looks up at the man in hope of a signal. The older dog displays no such histrionics, padding along behind in contented obedience. Once in the sea however, both dogs forego all sense of canine duty, leaping over each other and cavorting about like children. There is nothing quite as companionable as a dog.

Today's sea is flat calm. An otter is fishing in the voe directly below the house. I grab my camera and hurry out. Taking advantage of the thirty-second intervals in which the animal is under water I make it down to the sea wall without being sighted. Now it is just a matter of waiting.

After about ten minutes of watching this engaging little creature circle and dive in more or less the one spot, he suddenly makes a beeline for the rocky headland to my right. I must move quickly if I am going to reach the vicinity of where he will come ashore. He is staying close to the surface now, raising his head at five-second intervals. I have to cross an open beach with little hope of stealth.

With great good luck I manage to get into a concealed position adjacent to the otter's chosen landing spot. He hasn't seen me and is leisurely grooming himself behind some rocks making it possible for me to slowly narrow the gap between us. My way is over frost covered stones and seaweed. It is a tricky business. He may not see me but he'll hear me if I slip. Nearby, some gulls set up a plaintive mewing. It is a welcome noisy distraction as there is not a breath of wind and no other sound to cover any misplaced footfall.

The gulls fly off. Silence. I can see the otter's back above the rock shelf he is on. Suddenly he lifts his head and looks straight at me. I am about twelve yards away. My dark green jersey is providing good camouflage against the seaweed. Nevertheless, I think he has seen me, or perhaps picked up my scent. He continues grooming but is obviously nervous, keeping glancing in my direction. Most of his body is concealed from me and what photos I get are far from satisfactory.

This encounter has pretty much proved to me that my camera zoom is not sufficiently powerful for the purpose. I am unlikely ever to get closer than this unless I am lucky enough to come on a sleeping otter. Photos aren't everything. Being this close to a shy, wild animal is an exhilarating experience and one in which I count myself lucky.

Yet… what a difference a day can make. Yesterday's otter encounter is well and truly eclipsed by today's. Being on the lookout for my furry friend's possible return, I am soon rewarded and manage to position myself in a strategic spot close to where he is likely to come ashore. Sure enough, in he comes, carrying a good-sized lumpfish or "paidle" as they are locally known.

Creeping to the edge of the bank – the last few yards flat on my belly – I get into a position directly above my quarry. It is not long before he becomes aware of my presence but having started on his meal he's not about to abandon it without good reason. I take care not to unduly alarm him and am allowed to take several good photographs before quietly backing away and leaving him in peace. If I thought myself lucky yesterday, then today's experience is beyond words. *(See photo page v)*.

Heavy rain overnight has flushed out the last snow from deep gullies and turned every stream into a torrent. In the absence of sun, colours have been leeched from the landscape giving it an appearance of neglect. The only colour is in the marina where cheerily bright boats are moored. It seems that the flamboyancy that attends the painting of boats in Shetland seldom extends to people's houses, where (with few exceptions) a conservative uniformity prevails. Pebble-dash or stone-wash under a grey roof. Even attempts by some of the company-funded housing schemes to bring a touch of Norwegian gaiety have failed to stimulate the imagination, leaving these estates looking slightly incongruous in an otherwise monochrome environment. There are more colour variations amongst the sheep than amongst the houses!

A four-seasons-day and all of them different kinds of winter. From wild and woolly to creepy calm; drifting snow-flakes to bleak sunshine and fluky winds. A spring tide adds to sea's torment till it doesn't know whether it's coming or going.

It has been said the first light of day belongs to mountain tops, but the embryonic fluid out of which all life first emerged is the sea, and sun is born again from beyond its horizon each new day. Bursting out of the sea, it rises *gloriosus et libes*. And it is the sea into which it is laid to rest at day's end.

SEA VIEW

Whether in clear or clouded skies, sun is assured of a fanfare from the sea every morning and evening. Not even a peacock's tail can match the splendour with which sea heralds and dispatches the sun.

Catch of the day

When I was eight years old, I lived in Shetland. The village was called Walls.

There was an old stone pier where my pals and I met on fine Saturdays to fish and swap comics… *Desperate Dan, Beano, Phantom*….

Across from the pier was a 'Sweetie Shop' that also sold fish-hooks. In those days a penny could buy assorted merchandise. A fish hook cost a farthing, as did a variety of sweets. With a weekend penny at his disposal a boy had many choices.

Eventually, with a sweetie in one cheek and a spare fish-hook in my pocket, it was time to find some bait. Limpets were easiest. Hundreds of them clung to the pier-wall. Hooks loaded, we lay on the warm stones and lowered our lines into the oily black water between the rough stone wall and the hull of Mr Pole's trawler. All around us lay the detritus of a fishing village – broken barrels, old creels, coils of rope, upturned boats and bits of unidentifiable rusting junk.

A stone's throw away, on the far side of the harbour, a long, narrow wooden jetty built on stilts went all the way out to beyond the low-tide mark. At the end was a wooden privy. Sometimes we would see an old man heading out along the jetty and would nudge each other and wink. Spending a penny has other meanings besides buying sweeties! When the privy door closed, we'd watch for a tell-tale splash in the sea below so that we could derisively yell 'bomb's gone". (We were all *Biggles* fans.) Such diversions were few and far between, however, and in any case the main agenda was fishing.

On one occasion, when I saw the silver flash of a coalfish darting towards my bait, I stood up in excitement and leaned out too far. Next thing I knew I was plunging down into the icy water. I couldn't swim!

Rising to the surface, I let the fact be known in no uncertain terms…

"I can't swim!"

This had the desired galvanising effect on my pals who fortunately were all sons of the sea. While some grabbed spars to hold the boat from crushing me against the pier, my brother heaved a rope down. I was quickly hauled to safety.

Not so much a fish as a half-drowned rat.

(First published in *Shetland Life*, July, 2010)

That spring in my step as I climb the hill behind the house is being caused by more than sphagnum moss. With days stretching out and sun climbing ever higher into the sky, there is an air of optimism about the place. A feeling of *joie de vivre* coupled with deep contentment. Blue sea. Blue sky. Blissful calm. Shetland is turning on its irresistible charm and weaving a spell of entrapment. All who come here inevitably become enchanted and however much circumstances might

SEA VIEW

dictate the need for them to return to another place they will forever be compelled to return again and again. This is the magic of these islands. It is inescapable.

The old adage holds true: as the days lengthen, the cold strengthens. It snowed again last night and for the first time this winter (with only 10 days of the season left) there is substantial ice in the voe below the house. I suspect this is the result of minimum overnight temperature (-4 degrees) coinciding with low tide and low salinity caused by the nearby freshwater stream. Now, at 8.30am, with tide on the rise, ice has already broken into slurry and is drifting on the current. Despite a day of bright sun it is not enough to affect a thaw. We walk out on crisp snow trying to identify a variety of animal and bird footprints.

Family members visiting from Australia left heatwave conditions in Melbourne in search of a colder climate. They are getting a little more than they bargained for!

Yesterday's sea ice has expanded overnight, forming wide flows that are now drifting through the voe – at times black and at other times white under the changing light. It is easy to see how just a few more minus degrees could radically change this environment.

Our otter is back, catching sandeels between the pier and the links. He must be hungry as he fishes in the icy water for over an hour, providing a special treat for our visitors who are able to obtain some good photographs.

At 2.30pm the blizzard from Hell arrives. Families setting out for a Sunday drive (including several on their way to church) are forced to turn round and head for home. A few early birds actually make it to the kirk only to spend an anxious hour bedevilled by thoughts of being snowed in. Whose side is God on? Children who are unable to get to school tomorrow will probably reckon He's on theirs.

More snow in the night leads to the most extensive cover of the winter so far. During a lull, we decide to take a run down to Aywick where a council house is being readied for tenancy. It is one which we have a better than even chance of being allocated and so we are eager to see how the renovations are coming on. Workmen tell us they expect to be finished by 12th March. If we are lucky enough to get the house this would give us a window of two weeks to make the move from our current address in Mid Yell before our lease runs out. The notion of being homeless in the current weather conditions does not bear thinking about. (A little bird told me that.) The deprivations which small birds such as sparrows, finches, and Shetland's diminutive wrens, have to undergo to survive winter's sub-zero temperatures and harsh winds are such as to make me wonder how they manage. The avian population of mainland UK has the benefit of hedgerows and copses where they can generally find some cover. In Shetland's windswept environment, such havens are virtually non-existent. In the midst of yet another blizzard I watch one of these tiny birds (this time it's a finch) hopping between the pathetic twigs of a stunted and blasted willow and can only shake my head in disbelief that it might still be alive in the morning. Having a roof over one's head at this time of year is something to be truly thankful for. Continuing snowfall over the past few days has led to disruption of traffic movement in many parts of Shetland. Our Australian visitors have received the frozen equivalent of a baptism of fire. Not that they have complained. A picture-postcard landscape is providing endless photo opportunities. Everyone is talking snow-depth – eight inches here… twelve inches there. Wind has picked up and is driving the snow into drifts. I think of the animals. Where do rabbits find food in these conditions? And what of other species, how do they survive the arctic conditions? In all probability, many of them don't.

At 4pm, we receive a phone call from our newly departed visitors to advise us they have indeed experienced the frozen equivalent of a baptism of fire. On the way to Sumburgh airport and driving in a blizzard their car skids, leaves the road and does a 360-degree roll through a fence to land on its wheels. They walk away, shaken but otherwise unscathed. The car is not so fortunate, receiving extensive damage. This has been a day of exceptionally atrocious weather in Scotland with many similar accidents occurring throughout the country. Not all drivers will have been as lucky as my brother and sister-in-law.

Crap. Yes, I know, it appears to be a rather vulgar word with which to introduce a new subject but you may have noticed the absence of an exclamation mark. Furthermore, it might improve your opinion of me if I resort to the old spelling of krap, or better still krappin. The thing is, any preoccupation with sea in Shetland is inevitably going to lead to crap.

And now I must enlighten those who have no idea what I'm on about. Crap, or krappin, is a mixture of fish livers and oatmeal which is stuffed into a fish head and cooked in the oven. Once a staple of Shetland diet, it is still enjoyed by a goodly number today and is one of many such recipes that make use of fish offal of which there was once an abundance that would otherwise have gone to waste.

In the days before refrigeration when all fish exported from Shetland had to be salt pickled, air dried or smoked to preserve it, the process involved gutting the catch and cutting off the heads. Hundreds of Shetland men and women were employed at this task and were poorly paid. What would otherwise be discarded (especially the livers) became the workers' perks. A lowly fish-gutter could certainly eat as much as he or she wanted. Crappin (pronounce it crawpeen if it upsets your sensibilities) may not be to everyone's taste but it contains loads of lovely fish oil in an infinitely more palatable form than those highly expensive capsules you find in health food stores.

So, next time you are gutting your catch, think of crappin and take the livers home to cook. Haddock livers are best but cod or ling livers can also be used. There are oodles of good recipes. Margaret Stout's *Cookery for Northern Wives* (Reprint, Shetland Amenity Trust, 2008) has fifteen or more.

Four and a half hours of sunlight have been added to the equation since the shortest day. It is a time of year when the lengthening days are commonly remarked upon as everyone seeks to shrug off the burdensome coat of winter. No matter how cold it may be, spring is in the air and with it comes a new optimism.

SEA VIEW

My good friend Charlie sent me this fish soup recipe, which he describes as 'jumptastic'. There are no quantities given so I guess you just suit yourself.

Dice up your tatties (potatoes), neeps (turnips) and carrots. Half boil them in salted water. Drain off most of the water and add a tin of Carnation Milk. Re-heat but do not bring to the boil. Add chopped spring onions together with equal parts of fresh and smoked haddock broken into bite-sized pieces. Simmer for 10 to 15 minutes. Add a knob of butter then scoff till you are nearly bursting.

Cordon bleu chefs might scoff in a different way but as far as I'm concerned this is definitely 'jumptastic'. Quick and easy, too. Try it.

Draatsi. No, it does not mean "thank you" in Dar es Salaam. It is a Shetland dialect word, from the old Norn language, that was once used to describe a person or animal that walked with a heavy, shuffling gait. Nowadays it is the dialect word for an otter. Watching one just now as it makes its way across the snow, I smile at how aptly the word fits. This fellow is rolling like a drunken sailor as he heads down to the sea. Graceless on land they may be, but once in water they are in their element and become the epitome of streamlined litheness. I think this may be a different animal to the one I photographed. It is much darker against the pristine snow; almost russet in fact. Older looking, too. Two otters sharing my domain. How lucky is that? There can be little doubt this island is one of the best places for observing otters, though how many people are afforded multiple sightings without having to step outside their doors?

Next day, I wake to another blizzard. The long awaited thaw has been postponed yet again. Snow has featured on most days since mid-December and more often than not it has dominated to the point of obliterating all other considerations. It is time I looked at the bigger picture. I need to escape this blinkered existence and metaphorically sail out beyond the horizon. Sea, after all, is a global phenomenon.

There was a time when to have sailed the seven seas meant no more than the Mediterranean, Adriatic, Black, Red, Arabian and Caspian Seas with the Persian Gulf thrown in to make up the number. Nowadays one tends to think on a wider scale – Atlantic, Pacific, Indian, Mediterranean, Arctic, Caribbean and the Southern Ocean – these are modern man's Seven Seas though in fact there are around 100 to choose from. Even I can name my seven. Starting with the North Sea, I have also sailed through the Atlantic, Pacific, Indian, Mediterranean, Coral and South China seas. Not with a hand on the tiller you understand; more a chair on the promenade deck from where I can at least claim the view is more expansive (and frequently more expensive). Of course, I am fully aware that true blue mariners are unlikely to compare me with Sindbad (or any other of those intrepid sons of the sea who feature so largely in romantic literature) but, as the children's nursery rhyme puts it, I have been "three times round in my gallant, gallant ship" and so far have managed to avoid going "right to the bottom of the sea, the sea, the sea…"

50

SEA VIEW

With the vernal equinox (20th March) near at hand it comes as no surprise when I am wakened in the night by the first of its associated gales flinging hailstones at my windows with all the fury Boreas can muster. And in the morning Neptune is venting his spleen on the stoic rocks, battering them mercilessly with wave upon wave of his regimented armies.

It is a sunshiny day with just the right amount of cloud to animate the scene. Checking the view from the front window, I observe five rather large white birds in the middle of the voe. They appear to have their heads beneath the surface. Can't be whooper swans... wrong water. Too big for gulls. I put the binoculars on them. Five chunks of polystyrene foam! Bloody idiot! But they *looked* like birds – honestly.

I occasionally exchange emails with a yachtsman in the middle of the Atlantic. "We are now about 300 miles from St Helena and suffering from light weather. It's one in the morning. A lovely night with a bright but not quite full moon which has not managed to obliterate the Southern Cross or Orion. T shirt and shorts on a night watch. Oh, mercy, it's a hard life...". This is a man who has sailed into some of the remotest corners of the globe in his 42-foot, steel-hulled cutter. I envy him his intrepid spirit. I would not have the courage or tenacity, let alone the skill.

After lunch I am enticed out by brilliant sunshine, walking five miles through snow-clad hills where sub-zero temperatures have created a dazzling sheen that may be likened to tightly stretched silk. Though the snow is not particularly deep it is going to take several days of this weather to affect a thaw and at the moment sea seems to be achieving more than sun for it is only at its edge that the coast is clear, so to speak.

The thaw ('towe' or 'uplowsin' as Shetlanders call it) is under way once more. What sun and sea could not achieve between them is made easy by rain. Snow is quickly being stripped from the fields and hills, though it is still a work in progress. While it continues there will be little joy, what with the associated drop in temperature and all the slushy mess it creates. No one likes a thaw unless it relates to international relationships that have been frosty and are beginning to show signs of détente.

And, speaking of relationships, I note a restlessness amongst several species of birds as the urge to start breeding begins to take hold. Soon migrant flocks will be returning and then the raucous frenzy will be on in earnest as they jostle for nesting sites on the cliffs and beach heads.

Having been island-bound for the best part of three months, it is good to escape to the mainland of Shetland on another fine spring day. A ferry across Yell Sound and then a triangular journey through central mainland takes us west to Aith and Bixter; southeast to Lerwick then north to Yell once more. The thaw has left the landscape looking like a multi-ribbed skeleton. Every fold and wrinkle, every dip and hollow is delineated by deep snow while the rest is the yellowed, shrunken hide of a long-dead beast. Each cresting of a hill (no flat land here) brings a new seascape with long, probing fingers of water reminiscent of

SEA VIEW

Norway's fjords. Less dramatic, admittedly, but in this half-drowned land it is not hard to imagine how it might have looked a few millennia ago. Today's contours are softer, more enticing and with everything scaled down to diminutives. It is a land in which we are invited to go "peerie-wyes", which is to say softly, gently, cautiously. This is a fragile environment. We should treat it with respect.

Charlie returns from a couple of days fishing. He has been off with his brother at grounds known as the 'Burra Haaf' – somewhere between Foula and Fair Isle, I presume. He has a couple of bags of fillets for us. Four or five good feeds of haddock and monkfish tails – the latter worth £180 a box, he tells me. I stick my nose in the bag and inhale deeply. Fresh fish straight out of the Atlantic. My taste buds are dancing the Foula Reel. Fetch the frying pan.

It is to be hoped the world will never know a day when a man cannot go off in his boat and bring home such a meal to his family. And having stated it, I immediately recognise the naivety of such a remark for I know only too well that in many parts of the world this is already the case due to unscrupulous exploitation and greed.

The sea is everything. It covers seven tenths of the terrestrial globe. Its breath is pure and healthy. It is an immense desert, where man is never lonely, for he feels life stirring on all sides. (Jules Verne)

Makes you wonder why he then wrote about travelling "twenty thousand leagues" under it! Not the same thing at all, I'd venture to say, and certainly not in that inverted bathtub he dreamed up. Give me the sea, say I, but please don't wet my socks. And the only nautilus I am interested in is one I can hold to my ear in order to listen to marine music…

…*on the other hand, if there's an underlying core of poetry that I go to, I go to the sea…* or so said Richard Serra and I would have to agree with him. I set out on this 365-day journey with precisely that thought in mind. Sea is poetry in motion and when I become too old to walk its shore, I will sit on some metaphorical harbour wall and listen to its song.

Meanwhile, other things are beginning to crowd my mind as word comes that we have been allocated that house in Aywick – a tiny village with a big shop. And not only are we finally to have a house; we are to have our very own Sea View! A lifetime's longing brought to fruition. We can hardly believe our good fortune as there are plenty of council houses in Shetland that have no view at all, let alone one of the sea.

I am wakened by sounds of stuttering engines at the pier. Four of those jaunty red fishing boats are nudging one another like racehorses under starter's orders, impatient to be off. Victor's crane is ponderously lowering bundles of nets into waiting maws – a long-necked bird feeding its hungry chicks. Fishermen are purposefully moving about in lurid green striped oilskins. Each has a job to do and there is no wasted effort. Everyone wants to get going. One, two, three boats cast off their moorings and chug away, churning through the calm water.

SEA VIEW

A large inflatable dinghy roars out from behind the pier splitting and spitting white water. A moment later, a small aluminium one leaves and cleaves – this one even faster. Such urgency and eagerness to be at work! I'm willing to bet the pin-stripe-suited city slickers are not so quick, or slick.

Now the last boat is ready. This one is no beauty. A broad-hulled workhorse that is actually a cat (know what I mean?). For all its squat ugliness it can pirouette on a postage stamp. Away go the ropes. A last wave and it is gone. Victor's crane heads inland to its next job. It has taken a mere fifteen minutes of frenzied activity before all is done. Now, as the sea settles and gulls depart, nothing moves on or around the pier. I could tell myself it was all a dream except I know that somewhere beyond the headland fishermen have begun another day's work.

"Land is the most dangerous thing at sea". This quote, taken from *Then We Sailed Away* (co-authored by John Ridgeway together with his wife and daughter), seems to me to confirm what I have long suspected, namely that seafarers have an inherent dislike for terra firma. While I fully appreciate the implications of what the man says – why else would we have lighthouses – I still can't help wondering if he isn't writing from a thoroughly biased point of view. Yachties (correct me if I'm wrong) are so much in their element when at sea that fear takes a back seat. The steeper the waves the greater the adrenalin rush. How else could they return to it again and again? However, I do wonder if the most dangerous thing at sea is not, in fact, the sea. Ships may end up wrecked upon land but in most cases it is because the sea has driven them there. Then again, I have a feeling those same yachties will tell me the greatest danger man faces at sea is his own ignorance.

On a fresh and beautiful morning I propose a little excursion. Easy access to the outer isles of Unst and Fetlar is one of the perks of living in Yell and in both cases the ferries are free. We opt for Unst, a short hop across Bluemull Sound, which in turn is named after a spectacular headland on that island. My last visit to Unst took me to the far north region of Saxa Vord and Norwick. This time I am eager to explore in the vicinity of Snarra Voe and the Mull (pronounced Mool) which, to judge by the many ruins, must have been a heavily populated district at one time. The area appears to still have some of the best arable land on the island. It is a place of spectacular scenery dotted with ancient monuments including a large standing stone (12 ft high), the remains of a Norse farmstead and a massive broch. This first visit is by way of a reconnaissance. I will spend more time here when the long summer nights afford me the extra hours to explore. Already I can see that this is a truly beautiful place, having expansive views over North Yell to the far away Ramna Stacks (distinctive stacks out in the sea beyond Fethaland on Shetland's north mainland). From here, on midsummer's eve, I might watch what Shetlanders call the simmer dim or hümin as the sun tracks below the North Atlantic horizon for five hours or so before rising to another day. Or, on a winter's night, I might thrill to aurora borealis and wonder if this is Valhalla.

Our resident otters have been missing for a few days and inevitably we begin to wonder if they are okay, then at 10am the younger of the two comes trundling

SEA VIEW

up the middle of the road. A hooded crow decides to take a closer look and boldly hops right up. Whatever the otter said – and I doubt if it was complimentary – sets the bold one back on his tail feathers and he makes an undignified retreat. On comes Oscar (so named because we think his performances are worthy of one), right up the road until he is adjacent to our front garden at which point he ducks under the fence as if intending to drop in for a chat. He pauses briefly under the side window, allowing me to get a quick snapshot and then wiggles out under the back fence and on up the hill. Did he do all that just to please me?

I walk out along the pier every day now for soon I will leave this place and will have to make a slightly longer journey in order to obtain an ozone fix. Mid Yell pier is by no means a busy place as there is very little commercial trade going on aside from the servicing of the salmon farms and the comings and goings of a few fishing boats. There is always plenty evidence of these activities however – stacks of empty fish boxes, piles of nets, creels, mooring ropes and the usual detritus that seems to inevitably accumulate in the vicinity of piers in general. In particular, I like the fishy smell that permeates everything. It takes me back to my childhood in Walls where a smaller, older and much messier pier was one of my favourite haunts. When it comes to triggering memories, there is nothing quite as evocative as the tang of the sea… or the stink of dead fish!

Another encounter with Oscar results in some good photographs. It is a happy start to my day. After lunch, I set out for North-a-Voe aiming at a long circular walk to Kaywick and beyond. There is an almost eerie calm in the air and on the sea. Walking up the Burn of Markamouth, I come on the lovely little loch of Sigla Water cupped in the hills. Unlike many of Shetland's lochs which are stony-shored and devoid of bordering vegetation other than heather, this one has an extensive area of sedge making it an ideal place for nesting duck and other wildfowl. A place to visit later in the breeding season, perhaps.

Millennia of eroding rain and snow-melt has scoured the land. There is scarcely a flat piece of ground bigger than a dinner plate and much of what lies between is treacherously boggy. Lack of care might easily result in a twisted ankle – something to be avoided at all costs in these remote and forbidding hills. In concentrating on my footsteps, I fail to see an owl until it lifts into alarmed flight. It had been perched on a clump of moss not ten paces in front of me. Torn shreds of sphagnum mark the spot where it sprang aloft. Being no ornithologist I hesitate to make positive identification but what I watch in circling flight for a minute or more is certainly an owl. Its creamy white colour and mottled buff markings would seem to indicate a barn owl. A crow swoops to drive it off but the owl is more than a match for such aggression and the two adversaries fly side by side in a display of bluff and counter-bluff which the owl soon trumps with a sudden feint in which its outstretched talons are sufficient threat to make the crow veer sharply away and fly off. I crouch in the heather hoping the owl might alight nearby but it heads north over the hill and I am left to wonder at what this nocturnal bird was doing in the open hill in the middle of the day.

SEA VIEW

"Sun creeps up over the Coromandel Peninsula into the angel-eyed blue vault as a cool breeze kisses the Hauraki Gulf. Scudding puffs of clouds herald another fine morning. Still summer, yes, but shyly sighing into a long-awaited autumn... "

My New Zealand correspondent delivers his antithetical weather report from the antipodes where the thermometer continues to range in the high 20s. I think he wants to make me jealous. Does he succeed? Well... almost. You see, it is scarcely a fortnight since Her Majesty's Government deposited £50 to my account in consideration of a week of sub-zero temperatures. But, however evocative the picture he may paint (and I admit to a mind's-eye view of beautiful, sun-kissed Waiheke Island) nevertheless spring's tender promise is all about me and I know what is in store. At this latitude there is so much to look forward to in the coming season.

The song *Farewell to Yell* has a chorus line about the 'wilds o' Yell'. Today I explore a part of the island that seems to warrant this description. Leaving my car at the cattle grid south of Colvister, overlooking Basta Voe, I set out westwards towards the Loch of Lumbister. Peter Guy describes this walk in the Yell edition of his series *Walking the Coastline of Shetland* as "one of the most popular walks in Yell" although he fails to mention the interesting ruins of croft houses on the southern slopes above the loch.

The quality of the stonework in these ruins, along with remains of substantial steadings and a water mill, together with at least 10 acres of what has at one time been cultivated land, suggests a little hamlet of some substance existed here for many years. It would have been a lonely place in which to live. There is no sign of a road and the nearest stretch of coast is a good 20-30 minute walk away. I fail to make it as far as this so cannot say whether there is safe mooring where the Dale of Lumbister meets the sea. Apart from this spot, all else is high cliffs up and down the west coast. In the other direction (the one from which I have come), it would take an hour to reach Basta Voe on foot. It has always been said that Shetlanders were first and foremost fishermen, and this particularly applied to the population of Yell where most of the land is made up of agriculturally unproductive peat. The small amount of cultivation that has taken place over thousands of years of occupation is almost exclusively adjacent to the coast and especially around sheltered voes where a man might live within sight of his boat. It is surprising, therefore, to find these ruins so far inland. In fact, I doubt if any other habitation in Yell (if not the whole of Shetland) lies so far from the sea.

Despite these observations, I am drawn to the wild beauty of this place. In an increasingly overcrowded world, it would be tempting to turn back the clock and recreate what was once here. The large loch over which the ruins look has lovely little sandy beaches and is bound to be stocked with trout. Sea trout will travel up the picturesque Burn of Lumbister where it tumbles through that craggy dale. *(See photo page x)*. The mill will grind my corn and there is sufficient good and well-drained land to grow a few crops and keep a cow. If (as I suspect) the narrow mouth of the Burn of Lumbister could keep a boat safely noosted during summer, then I will have fish aplenty. I might return here later in the season and explore that enticing valley, which Peter Guy tells us abounds in juniper, honeysuckle, roseroot and heather, and if I find it all to my liking, well, who knows, I might lock in my reincarnation preferences.

"The sea complains upon a thousand shores" (Alexander Smith) and today it has good reason. Restless gulls warn us of an impending storm and by mid-day it is beginning to make itself felt, rattling the gate and buffeting the gable end of the house. Although it is gusting to 65 mph, were it not for the noise I might be fooled into thinking it was less severe, as wind from this direction does not impact as dramatically upon the voe as a south-easterly or northerly. Nevertheless, sea *is* complaining upon the shore and all the gulls are grounded.

Nearing the day when we are to move house I realise we will miss the view from this place and of course we will miss Oscar! To tell the truth however, I think I would find the slightly blinkered outlook onto what is more often than not a rather cosseted voe would eventually stifle me. I forever want to see what is round the corner. Each day I watch the little fishing boats head out of sight and fancy I'd like to follow them. At the new house there will be a wider view to open sea and distant islands. On stormy days we will be treated to the full force of whatever the elements care to throw at the cliffs we look out upon. It will be a 'sea view' with no holds barred. In other respects, it is a smaller community with very few comings and goings – certainly no pier with its associated activity. Fortunately, the better weather and longer days are going to make it possible for me to get out and about more and for the foreseeable future there is lots of exploring to do. I will be within walking distance of some truly spectacular cliffs where gannets, guillemots and puffins will shortly be nesting. Yes, it is going to be an interesting time.

A day of brilliant sunshine has me grabbing my Ordnance Survey 'Explorer' map number 407 and heading out to the head of Basta Voe from where it is about an hour's hike beyond the Knowes of Bratta to the west coast. I am determined to return to Dale of Lumbister and check out the lie of the land there but first I have to negotiate the boggy hills in between. Walking Shetland's hills takes twice as long as to walk a comparable distance along the coast. Forget the shortest distance between two points! Hill walking can be an extremely frustrating and convoluted business as you try to pick your way between myriad tiny tarns and over the treacherous burns that seem to cut through everywhere. In places, I hear the gurgling chuckle of running water but on approaching the deep clefts where the sound is coming from I find that the stream is nowhere to be seen. Having worn its way deep into the hill it has become overgrown by turf and heather. To step into one of these gullies could be a dangerous business as I might easily fall through to the cavern below.

Reaching the coast after an hour's heavy trudging, I find spectacular cliffs that are woven through with veins of pink and white quartz. Turning south I head for the Dale of Lumbister, the entrance to which is marked by a cairn on Gorset Hill, 275 feet above the crashing waves. Tiny waterfalls tumbling over the cliffs are being blown upwards and inland by a strong westerly wind. The dale itself is a place of wild beauty where the sea cuts in through a narrow geo at the mouth of Whalfirth to meet the sparkling Burn of Lumbister. The place is all that I had hoped for and a striking feature in a majestic landscape where loch and hill create harmonious balance.

Ex libris has taken on a whole new meaning for me. The Shetland Library van comes to my door once a month with an excellent choice of books and I can borrow several at a time. Not surprisingly, the largest category on offer is what I call 'mushy romances' to meet the demands of the many elderly widows in this community. These take up nearly a third of the van's shelving (the books, not the widows – though I get the impression some of the latter would happily move in and become bookworms in residence). Next most popular are books about the sea – fact, fiction, drama, adventure, marine biology, exploration, fishy stories, famous voyages, piracy, deep-sea diving and much more including many written by Shetlanders. Clearly this is a favourite topic in these sea-girt islands where many readers are themselves retired seamen of one type or another. Resolved (as I am) to write something on the subject every day for a year, is it any wonder I am in rhapsodies? Where else outside of a university would one be so generously provided with research material on this scale? There is plenty to dive into – both shallow and deep – some of it uncharacteristically dry and some decidedly wet. My sea view has expanded far and beyond the range of my 10x50 binoculars. I am in the swim.

A flick back through the pages confirms my memory that March came in like a lion. Can I presume it will go out like a lamb? With five days to go I may be jumping the gun but if today should be taken as an indicator then it will not only be a lamb-ending but a lame-lamb one. It is what east-coast Scottish dwellers call a haar, or what others call a Scotch mist. If you add dreich to the equation – another good old Scots word meaning cheerless, dismal or dreary – then you are beginning to get the picture. Not that I am complaining. Being in the midst of packing, preparatory to a temporarily move off the island while awaiting the keys to our new home in Aywick, neither the weather nor the view is uppermost in my mind. Less so because the latter is non-existent through the former. Yes, a dreich haar pretty much sums it up.

I believe it was the Chinese who first utilised magnetic properties in certain types of stone to invent the compass. What became known as lode (lead) stone was suspended amidships, well clear of any iron to guide their epic voyages beyond the horizon where no man had ever gone before. We may conjecture the extent to which they depended upon this rather crude navigational aid but one thing is apparent; their ability to conquer the sea went unchallenged for many centuries before the Vikings took to plundering on a grand scale.

Temporarily back on the island of Bressay for a week or so, my sea view is a tantalising distant triangle through which the island's ferry passes on her regular trips to and from Lerwick. I will have to walk to the lighthouse if I am to have a

SEA VIEW

proper view. A bitter northerly wind that is the harbinger of more snow almost has me turning tail and returning to the cosy house. Persistence pays off, however, as it is not quite so cold once I reach a sheltered hollow near the lighthouse and the cliffs here are sufficiently spectacular to make me forget my freezing ears. *(See photo page x)*.

Next day we return to Yell for a compulsory viewing of our new house. The predicted snow comes flurrying in on the back of force seven winds making driving conditions hazardous. It also makes a mockery of that "out like a lamb" prediction (unless it's to do with the fleecy ground-cover). More particularly, I am reminded that this is the last of the 'borrowing days' when, according to old Scottish folklore, April borrows the last three days from March and each one sets a pattern for weather in the ensuing three months. The Spanish version of 'borrowing days' tells of a shepherd who promised March a lamb if he would bring soft winds to suit the flock. After his request was granted, the shepherd reneged on his promise and in revenge March borrowed three days from April in which to send fiercer winds than March ever delivered. Either way, it does not augur well for the coming months. The house is nice, however, and our sea view, even through driving rain, is very appealing. I have already decided where to position my chair. Now, if the contractors could just get a few days of reasonable weather to finish the outside paths, we might be able to move in and start unpacking.

Back we go to Lerwick and another session at the housing department as we try to establish an entry date for our new house. Still no joy. Sometimes you need the patience of a saint when dealing with bureaucracy. Meanwhile there is furniture and kitchen appliances to be bought and when that is done there is a busy harbour scene to enjoy on a fine afternoon. No doubt the bureau-crazy will get their paper clips untangled in the next week or so and we will get the keys to our Aywick sea view.

An early start in bright sunshine has me overlooking the narrow passage (Noss Sound) between Bressay and Noss before 8am. It is here I record my first twitcher of the season – a yellow-coated male of the species. It is possible this one may have become disorientated while searching for a mate as it is wandering in circles close to the landing stage on Noss with no visible means of support. I resist the temptation to hail it. Twitchers can be a flighty breed, easily ruffled and prone to irrational behaviour. Given this one's location a good month before the expected arrival of its primary stimulation, I decide to ignore it. Come to think of it, my own presence in this out-of-the-way spot could easily be misconstrued by others. I decide that a dignified retreat is called for and go home to boiled duck eggs for breakfast. After all, it *is* Good Friday so eggs seem appropriate.

Ferried across the harbour in drifting rain, I head to the Shetland Museum and Archives where the display includes various types of traditional Shetland boats including sixareens, the clinker-built six-oared vessels of the haaf or deep-sea fishing of yore. The lighter, more rakish version of these boats is known as a yoal. Where the heavy sixareen requires a man for each oar, yoals can be. rowed by three men wielding two oars apiece. Smaller four-oared boats known

58

as fourareens are also on show. Several classic Shetland boats are suspended in a specially designed three-storey loft making it possible to view them from below as well as from above. The museum is located on Lerwick's oldest reconstructed dock where a number of vessels are in situ including a herring drifter and other fishing boats. While there are all manner of displays relating to Shetland's long and colourful history, it is readily apparent that the sea has featured uppermost in the life of the islanders in every age.

Easter Sunday. I might have joined the dwindling faithful and gone to church except this year I fancy a different sort of communion. Parking the car at the lighthouse, I set off to climb the lower slope of The Ward (known as South Hill) where it falls away to high cliffs at the southern extremity of Bressay. It is here over a thousand years ago that hermit priests lived in cave-like cells on a grassy ledge halfway down the cliff. Finding the ruins, I sit in wonderment at what can possibly have inspired men to subject themselves to such deprivation. Was it a kind of self-denial or penance imposed by their superiors? How did they survive here and what did they eat? On a day like today, when the sea is shining and there is only a light breeze to ruffle its surface, one could easily escape into a trance and feel blessed. Sun is warming my back and cloud shadow is dancing across an awesome scene where cliff, sea and sky fill my world. But there is much more to this place than these elements alone. When I shift my focus, I see life stirring in every nook and cranny. Fulmars are pairing off on the ledges above me in preparation for the breeding season. Buds are swelling on the fat clumps of sea-pinks (thrift) at my feet and new shoots are greening in nearby heather. Far below on the burnished sea, hundreds of gulls are congregated like a fleet of tiny white-sailed yachts waiting for the starter's gun. Yes, on a fine day like this, a resident hermit might happily conclude that God is in his heaven and all is well. At other times – say in a south-easterly gale – this place would be a veritable hell. What price a hermit's life then? And would he as easily find his God?

I contemplate a hermit's life on the cliffs of Bressay.

After two days of atrocious weather it is nice to wake to blue skies. I am up and out good and early, starting at the lighthouse and heading north. Sea is deep blue and what is termed confused, though whether by tide or changing winds I couldn't say – probably both. The coast here consists of low cliffs and steep little geos with the occasional stony beach. A couple of small caves and mini sea-arches add a touch of the dramatic, setting my fertile imagination into overdrive as I envisage unscrupulous men in bygone days using lanterns to lure merchant ships onto the rocks. Bressay's gain

SEA VIEW

being Lerwick's loss. And across the sound that so called 'Venice of the North' glints in the sunlight, its busy harbour waking to commerce. But I have smaller fish to fry. In a hook-shaped geo named the Cro of Ham I find some interesting jetsam. No barrels of rum, but some nice planks of wood I'm sure I can find a use for. My first bit of productive beachcombing. I'll probably end up carting it all the way up to Yell. Thus encumbered I cut short my walk at Ham Voe where an over-zealous gander warns me to keep clear of his mate who is sitting on her nest in a rather exposed piece of the beachhead.

In the afternoon we head into Lerwick and I return to the museum to photograph some of the boats in the dock. Many were working vessels in their day and somehow this arbitrarily imposed and permanent mooring seems like a fall from grace. Later still, I go in search of some older boats which I am told are at the beach below the house on Bressay where I am staying. These latter are particularly poignant and their sturdy craftsmanship is self-evident though they are no longer seaworthy. I fancy they have served their owners well and are far from being banished or neglected; they are noosted here along with their old winch to rot and rust in peace.

A drive to Nesting and Gletness on Mainland Shetland's east coast takes us through scenery that looks scaled down – a *papier mâché* setting through which a model railway might run. Even the already diminutive Shetland ponies are smaller in this district. I swear I've seen bigger stuffed toys and the picture postcard cottages tucked in against rocky outcrops look as if they could be picked up and rearranged at will. It is a Lilliputian landscape. And through it all, up, over and around miniature hillocks, the narrow road winds to reveal an ever-changing vista into which sea encroaches in myriad torturous tentacles. Where sea ends, silver streamlets twist down fairy glens connecting penny-farthing lochs with one another. In every cove and sheltered corner, peerie boats lay huddled together waiting for adventure; for this is a place where no man could resist the pull of the sea. Gletness in particular is arguably one of the prettiest spots in Shetland with all the tiny islands beyond it just begging to be explored.

This is a red-letter day! We are to sign up and receive keys to our new home! Our appointment at Shetland Islands Council housing department is mid-morning and consequently by the time the paperwork is completed it is too late to organise delivery of furniture etc. Tomorrow is another day (as my father used to say) so back to Bressay we go.

There being only one remaining section of Bressay's coastline that I have not traversed on either this visit or the earlier one last September, now is the time to complete the circuit. After lunch, I drive across the island to make good the gap. Parking the car above the Voe of Cullingsburgh, beside a chortling burn on which are the remains of two little corn mills, I am reminded of how efficiently the early crofters made use of autumn rains in these situations, turning multiple water wheels one below another in the same stream. It is evidence of how populated these now empty moors once were. A little further along the coast I come on an interesting historical graveyard and the ruins of a medieval church. The remains of a broch on the same site is evidence of even earlier habitation. It is in this region that an elaborately carved Pictish stone known as the Cullingsburgh or Bressay Stone was discovered around 1852. It all adds up to many centuries of occupation – Picts, Celts, Vikings. If only the stones could speak, what a tale they could tell. But like so much of Shetland, this is now a silent place frequented only by sheep and the occasional hiker like myself.

Reaching the most easterly point of the island (Rules Ness) beyond which lies a wide expanse of open sea, I rest for a while listening to the frush of half-hearted waves that scarcely have the energy to stagger ashore. To my south lies the wedge shaped island of Noss, its spectacular east-facing cliffs hidden from view. I have been promised a boat trip there in summer when the gannet and guillemot rookeries will be full and puffins will be in residence on the cliff tops. If the Noss episode in Simon King's TV documentary is anything to go by then I am in for a treat.

A four-ferry day. Charlie and I head off to Yell with a load of household goods in Big Ivor's van. Correction: it is a *five*-ferry day because besides crossing Bressay and Yell Sounds twice we also ferry a load of boxes from Mid Yell to Aywick. It is on days like this that you discover who your friends are. I could not have managed on my own.

The only respite comes during the ferry trips. Some would count them as an inconvenience but I consider ferries (apart from never being quite the same from one day to another) to be the vital links in the chain that makes Shetland a homogenous community rather than a disconnected scattering of islands. To me, inter-island travel is one of the special attractions of living here.

And now we have just one last day on Bressay before the BIG MOVE. Hoping to find some early-arrival puffins I climb to the highest point overlooking the sea at south Bressay – a spot called the Mills of Ord – only to be met with raucous clamour. Every available ledge seems to be occupied. What a difference a week can make. Cliffs that were virtually silent last Sunday are now teeming with birds. What is the collective noun for fulmars? A fractiousness? That hermit's tranquillity I was envying on my last visit has well and truly vanished. Living in the midst of this constant bickering might threaten my sanity. It reminds me of an occasion when I stayed for a time in a beachfront holiday house on Phillip Island in Victoria, Australia. I was in the middle of a shearwater rookery with several pairs in burrows under the house. With nesting space at a premium the squabbling went on all night. Talk about domestic violence! In the end I took to sleeping during the afternoon while the adult shearwaters were out at sea and their grotesquely fat chickens were dosing. And by the way, although puffins are reported to have returned to Sumburgh on Shetland's southern coast, they are not yet on these cliffs.

Back on the ferries once more, only this time it is a one-way trip. We are going to take possession of our new home! Needless-to-say there is very little time for indulging in sea views… yet on arrival I cannot keep from glancing out the front

SEA VIEW

window just to be sure the view is still there. And between times I keep pinching myself to be certain I'm not dreaming.

Ever since I first left the shores of Shetland in 1950, the longing to return and live within sight of the sea has never left me. How true Jacques Cousteau's words are – words I chose for the flyleaf of this writing: "The sea, once it casts its spell, holds one in its net of wonder forever". And at last it is mine again.

It takes three days to get sorted out; taking delivery of furniture flat-packs plus cooker, fridge, washing machine, lounge suite, beds, table, chairs and all the other paraphernalia considered essential to modern living. Without the help of good friends Peter and Rae we would be physical wrecks. We could never have done it without them. And in the midst of our frenzied activity the sea remains uncharacteristically calm, reassuring me that tranquillity awaits just as soon as I can get that last box unpacked...

... and then it is all done. The pictures are hung, the crockery and crystal unpacked (praise be, none of it is broken), clothes are hanging in the wardrobe and I have found my slippers. Now to pour a dram, settle in that comfy chair by the window (binoculars near at hand) and drink in the view.

Directly below the hillock on which our house is situated, at about 500 yards distance, the sea smiles up at me out of Ay Wick. A little further out is the craggy headland known as The Poil *(see photo page xi)*. I first met this view six months ago when I wrote "I could cheerfully end my days here in blissful contentment". And now here I am. Can I really be this lucky? From my elevated position I can also see north across the Loch of Vatsetter to the distant island of Unst. It is a wide panorama that takes in the length of Fetlar over which the sun rises. I will not tire of this view should I live to be a hundred.

> *When the captain walked the quarterdeck, no sailor ever thought of passing on the weather side. If going to or from the wheel, they always went on the lee side, or if a sailor had work to do on the weather side, he would, in passing, touch his cap in salute and pass to leeward, never going between the captain and the wind.*
> **Rose Cottage,** Oliver W. Cobb; Reynolds De-Walt (1968)

I came across this quote in something I was reading the other day and was reminded of the many seemingly quirky customs and superstitions of seamen. Presumably there was some practical reason for this. Was it that by going to windward a crewman might be blown against his captain and cause him to fall overboard? Or (perish the thought) might he be tempted to push him?

With our boxes unpacked (some that have been in store for a considerable number of years), we find we have two ships in bottles, a box-framed model schooner and several plates, tapestries and photos featuring ships. Anyone would think we were old salts. All that is needed to complete the image is a telescope on a tripod,

SEA VIEW

though with a pair of binoculars on the front windowsill (every Shetland home has them) the impression is pretty much the same. Perhaps I should purchase a stuffed parrot on a perch to stand in the corner, or would that be going too far?

I have been seated at the front window for the greater part of today watching the play of light along the cliffs of Fetlar, which are approximately four miles away. At times they seem much closer. I had originally fancied the idea of living in Bressay where I could watch all the comings and goings in Lerwick harbour but there is something infinitely satisfying and peaceful about this more expansive view through which boats scarcely ever pass. Doubtless, there will be a little more activity in summer and winter's storms will not leave me short of action.

Sun is already climbing into the sky when I set out at 6am. Heading south from behind the house I am soon at Otterswick where I greet my new neighbour, the White Wife (the ship's figurehead I met here some months ago). She is not very neighbourly, standing with her nose in the air. I'll get no juicy gossip from this one and in any case it is much too cold to be standing in idle chatter. Continuing south round the voe I reach Gossabrough then cut inland to the road and head home. A two-hour round trip with snow on the ground and a knife-edged wind threatening to cut off my ears. What kind of fool am I when everyone else is still sanely tucked up in their beds?

The main islands of Shetland are set in an elongated pattern running north and south. Unst is the most northerly, with Fetlar directly under it about four miles further south. The slightly larger island of Yell is offset to the south-west of these with a long sea corridor running between the three through which northerly or southerly weather tends to be channelled. Sitting in my eyrie, I can watch this heavenly drama being played out as cloud banks are funnelled down, spilling rain or chasing sun along the cliffs of Fetlar. On a day of alternating weathers such as today, when snowy showers periodically obliterate the scene, it is a source of perpetual delight as the sun moves across the sky to create changing angles of light on the high cliffs below Gallow Hill on Fetlar, or nearer at hand when it floodlights The Poil, so that every rock feature stands out in sharp relief.

By next day only a thin pencil line of gold marks the horizon; all else is dirty dishwater grey. It is raining. Even as I watch, the pencilling is being rubbed out, turning my optimism to pessimism. Fat chance of fair weather, especially as I have been looking east and it is all doom and gloom in the weather quarter which is north. Happily, I have an Ian Rankin (Rebus) novel with which to while away the day. It is appropriately titled *Set in Darkness*. Not being very good at unravelling plots it will probably take me to the last page before I see the light. Meanwhile a dirty day turns progressively dirtier – if one can refer to snow in these terms. The flurrying flakes go past horizontally in total disregard of gravity. Is this something to do with that erupting volcano in Iceland upsetting the earth's equilibrium? It reminds me of the old lady lamenting unseasonably foul weather during the war and declaring "it's aa thae booms". She was firmly of the opinion that dropping bombs made holes in the sky and so upset the weather. Could be she had a point.

I was wrong about the paucity of boats in this region. It appears to be quite a popular fishing ground. A little prawn-boat is busily circling just off The Poil and a couple of others are working south of Fetlar. Colgrave Sound may not compete with the English Channel but it is certainly a shipping lane of sorts and it looks like the binoculars will be in regular use. I may even be persuaded to neglect the garden in favour of boat-spotting. And besides, who needs rhubarb when there is the possibility of an orca-sighting?

Footsteps…
Neatly placed and evenly paced
Strike obliquely o'er the sand.
A man and his dog have passed this way
From dunes to sea rim's strand.

Keel marks…
Deeply breach within ocean's reach
Cut uniquely thru sea foam
For man and his dog have sailed away
And I am left alone

An early start to the day has me heading north along the road for half a mile before striking out across the moor in the direction of the Birrier near Vatsetter. After a week of atrocious weather in which rain, sleet and snow has kept me somewhat confined, it is good to get out once more. Anyone watching me zigzagging around the sodden hollows and ice encrusted tarns would take me for a drunkard. There is substantially less dry land than wet in this hill and sometimes I seem to be going in circles. Eventually I make it to the coast where the walking is always easier. As on Bressay a couple of weeks ago, the cliffs are teeming with fulmars. No sign of any other breeding sea-birds however. Can't say I am surprised. Last week was more like midwinter than spring. Any self-respecting prospective cliff tenant would be well advised not to take up residence yet a while.

Next day is one of summer warmness under a blanket of mist that all but obliterates any view of the sea. By mid-afternoon it is possible to see glimpses of blue (both sea and sky) through what is now a moth-holed shawl. Yet it clings, unwilling to be cast aside, and as the day wears out the holes are repaired and we are left as mystified as we started … and another day of the same. Sombre sea appears to be calm but a long swell translates to bursting surf on the black rocks of The Poil. It is the only animation in a dumbed-down day. My father used to say "improve the shining hour", but what if it isn't shining? Ah well, never mind the hour – shining or otherwise – I'll improve the garden instead. The veggie patch needs digging… and *still* needs digging. I am not saying I chickened out yesterday, despite there being a good deal of rain to provide adequate excuse. No, I actually *did* do some digging but I think I've discovered why this place is called 'Steenbrae'. The ground is full of steens or more properly stanes (stones). Rocks might be a better word or even boulders! A man would need a crowbar and dynamite to turn this sodding soil. Am I really that desperate to grow my own vegetables? No! … but wait. Maybe if I slowly chip away at it (so to speak). After all, I've got nothing else to do. With time on my side I might achieve some sort of minor miracle. Improve my carbon footprint. Plant a tree for some future delinquent George Washington to chop down. And if I dig out enough rocks (a virtual certainty if yesterday's square yard is anything to go by) I might build a folly to rival some of the brochs around here. Come to think of it, maybe that is what those brochs are all about. Neolithic man trying to prepare enough ground to grow a cabbage.

Still preoccupied with gardening, I've put out the word that I'm in the market for cuttings and the like. One thing we are never likely to be short of is rain! We don't even have an outside tap! And the car cleans itself in the wind-driven horizontal rainstorms that would rival any car-wash. The minister called to see us today and in discussing the weather he commented that when the wind stops blowing everyone seems to grow in stature by two or three inches. A succinct observation. There is nothing like a Shetland blizzard to make you pull your head in! And I was amused to hear that the local shop sold out of hair-dryers last week. The crofters were all buying them to dry their new-born lambs! What gets me is the inordinate amount of fuss that is made over these 'hameaboot' lambs (the ones in the small fields around the houses) while the hill sheep are left to their own devices no matter how bad the weather is. It seems the native Shetland sheep (the ones in the hills) are made of sterner stuff than imported breeds such as Suffolks, Leicesters and the like. Diminutive as indigenous Shetland sheep are, they are tough little blighters with a good instinct to take cover in inclement weather. There is a ruined steading behind our house and I frequently see them crowding in through its doorway when it's raining or blowing a gale.

Much as I love my new home, I must admit to some initial disappointment in having to leave Oscar behind in Mid Yell. Imagine my delight therefore in walking out this evening and seeing a *pair* of otters cavorting together at no great distance from the house. As they are almost certainly a breeding pair, I hope to make their acquaintance over the coming months. Could be I will have some exciting times ahead.

At 10.00pm the door opens and our neighbour walks in. "Brought you a fry," he says, handing Adaline a bag of fillets to select from. She fetches a plate and chooses a couple to which our benefactor promptly adds a couple more. Two meals of freshly caught haddock the like of which only a privileged few ever get to taste. There are no words to describe it although 'epicurean ecstasy' might come close. Housewives in Scotland's fishing villages have an inkling of what it is like to eat freshly caught fish as the ones they buy have not long left the sea and have passed through few hands. In the big industrial cities further south people are less fortunate and must resort to sauces and condiments to enhance (or disguise) the taste. Even here in Shetland, where it was once commonplace for a proportion of the freshly landed catch to be distributed freely amongst neighbours, it is now a rare treat to be given a fry in this manner and all the more special for that. Expertly filleted and ready for the pan, a pinch of salt and

SEA VIEW

a squeeze of lemon is all that is required to turn this into a feast fit for a king. A one-time Shetlander, Ethel Hoffman, wrote a book she titled *Mackerel at Midnight* (Camino Books, Philadelphia, 2005) in which she describes an occasion when the men of the house rowed off late at night to catch a few fish which the women promptly set to and fried – mackerel at midnight. It still happens.

It is early morning and too soon to say whether mist will give way to sunshine or vice versa. Where flocks of birds were the norm a couple of months ago, now they make their way about in pairs, some noisily defending territory, others furtive, as if they might have a nest nearby. There are gannets diving in the voe, turnstones busy at the ebb, hooded crows staking a claim on a cliff edge, duck and geese overhead, and bright-beaked oystercatchers everywhere.

The beach at Salt Wick is covered with handy-sized and beautifully formed stones of glistening quartz. I figure if I take a few home every time I pass this way there will soon be enough to create an attractive feature in the garden. Having made a selection I turn inland aiming at a shortcut over the Hill of Queyon to Steenbrae. It proves to be anything but short. The Hampton Court Maze would be infinitely easier to negotiate than this stretch of sodden moor.

I've read folktales of men vanishing without trace in these hills; their disappearance attributed to malevolent trows or to some bottomless sinkhole in the middle of a marsh. I fancifully imagine the coroner's inquiry into the discovery of my body six months hence. There is much speculation in the press when it is revealed that my pockets were full of stones. Was this a case of murder – the body weighted and dumped in the bog? Or did the victim deliberately choose to take his own life, knowingly filling his pockets with stones to ensure he would sink below the surface? A secretive man who walked alone and kept a strange diary. Why had he crossed the world to live in this remote spot? Had any strangers been sighted in the region around the time of his disappearance? The coroner's patience would have been sorely tried by outrageous and unsubstantiated rumours, innuendo and blatant lies. In the end he would wisely bring in a verdict of "death by misadventure", adding a codicil that to go walking through boggy ground in Shetland with pockets full of stones is little short of lunatic behaviour.

I make it home with nothing worse than wet feet. For the time being the stones go on the windowsill. I'll have worn out my pockets long before I have accumulated sufficient material to create anything of note. Now I have *two* follies on the drawing board.

On a brighter, cheerier day, we head to Burravoe where the Scottish Women's Rural Institute (SWRI) are holding a plant sale. It's a case of "first come, best served" and we rush round the hall gathering up a variety of hardy, wind-resistant perennials. The best plants to grow in Shetland gardens are those that can withstand the icy winds that blow in off the sea. Plants that have come out of someone else's garden and already proved their worth are a safe bet. After a couple of trips to the car with boxes of excellent specimens, the good ladies take pity on me and start *giving* me more. I end up with the car's hatchback loaded to

SEA VIEW

the gunnels. Back at Steenbrae (where the wind never stops blowing) and with a bag of compost to help things along, I set about creating an instant garden in the certain knowledge that if anything will grow this lot will. I haven't the foggiest notion what the majority of the plants are, although I recognise a couple of species – perennial poppies, daphne, lamb's ears (my dictionary tells me it is actually *stachys byzantina*) and fuchsia. This latter provides good ground-cover. That much I do know! An hour later the work is done. Now to sit back and watch it grow – or blow out of the ground!

A clockwise turn round the Ness of Queyon seems destined to become a favourite walk in the months ahead. The shorter version, cutting back up the hill to Steenbrae, takes a little over an hour while the longer route, which passes the White Wife and incorporates Otterswick, requires closer to two hours. Today I opt for the shorter way, passing a small tarn near the hilltop where I encounter my seasonal first pair of red-throated divers. Rated amber on the RSPB list (meaning not exactly endangered but nevertheless under special protection) it is inadvisable to approach breeding pairs and one should not attempt to photograph their nests. Consequently, I will be giving this pair due consideration in the coming months and leaving them in peace.

At last I have a day of suitable weather to pay another visited to the Horse of Burravoe. I have now hiked there from opposite directions and so can state that the northerly approach (from Gossabrough) appears to me to be the quicker of the two. Having heard that puffins returned to Sumburgh about four weeks ago, I fully expect to find some in residence at The Horse. Crossing a high point on the moor, I am met by a great skua, or bonxie, as Shetlanders name them. This is a lone bird, probably newly arrived at its choice of breeding ground and awaiting a mate. Where many nesting birds will dive at intruders, the fiercely aggressive skua frequently goes one further, striking unprotected heads with its outstretched feet and drawing blood from the unwary. So far, this bird has nothing more to defend than its choice of breeding ground and so its tentative swoops are more in the way of practice runs and pose no threat. I continue on, unimpeded. There is a fresh wind blowing out of the north and the temperature is only four or five degrees but there is sunshine on my face and plenty of blue sky. Perfect hiking weather and I am at the Horse within half an hour, climbing the steep slope that is its fat rump, up to the saddle (which is only about 25 paces wide) and down to the head where the puffins should be – except they are not. On another day I might have been disappointed, but this is such a beautiful spot and such a beautiful day, I sit on the cliff top for fifteen minutes or so, surrounded by a ballet of skimming fulmars, and breathe the freshest air in the world. I cannot think to be anything other than happy to be alive.

More often than not, I go hiking alone. According to some people, being alone equates with being lonely. Not so. The solitude affords an opportunity for introspection. An Australian cartoonist named *Leunig* used to draw pictures of a strange little man who was supposed to represent his alter-ego. In place of his navel he drew a window through which he peered into himself from time to time.

SEA VIEW

Walking alone in remote places; going at one's own pace and being answerable to no one allows us to do this to some extent; discover who we are. It is a discovery we all need to make at some point in our lives.

With the ever-lengthening days it is as feasible to set out for a hike at 6pm as at 6am and this is precisely what I do today, on a bright sunny evening. A short drive takes me to where I park above the crescent of white sand at the Wick of Gossabrough, for a short walk along the coast north towards Otterswick and back. On the bank above the beach I unexpectedly come upon a cormorant which I presume is ailing, or possibly injured, as it makes no attempt to fly away. Not wishing to alarm it unduly, I let the zoom lens of my camera do the close encounter stuff and come away with several good photos which I could not possibly have obtained under normal circumstances. I am surprised to discover just how large this bird is; over 2ft in length by my estimate and with remarkably sturdy legs. When I return an hour later, it has gone.

In recognition of yesterday's opening remarks, I am out at 6.15 this morning. Sea is calm and luminescent and there is an expectant hush in the keen air. I've never seen so many rabbits. At this early hour the countryside is alive with them. A small flock of eider duck have arrived in the voe. A curlew is trilling its rippling call out on the moor behind me, disturbing the peace in the nicest way. In marshy ground and along the margins of ditches clumps of yellow iris (*Iris pseudacorus*) (referred to as seggi-flooers by Shetlanders) are beginning to show forth. Now a few inches high, they will soon reach to my waist and provide perfect cover for nesting wildfowl. Out on the cliff edge pink buds of thrift are swelling. The coming weeks will see a proliferation of growth as virtual endless daylight urges all of nature to make hay while the sun shines. Meanwhile there is a garden to be dug. I collect three more stones from Salt Wick beach and head home for breakfast.

Tirricks (Arctic terns) have returned to Shetland. The most travelled of all migratory birds; they are equally at home in Antarctic regions, returning here to breed in the spring and crowding out beachheads wherever they can scrape a nest in the sand. They are my favourite bird despite being stridently noisy and fierce defenders of their territory. Artful as swallows in flight; swooping, dipping and skimming across the sea's surface to catch tiny fish, their aerial acrobatics are always a delight to watch. I think all Shetlanders (who call them tirricks in imitation of their alarm call) love them because they are such cheerful harbingers of summer and their departure in autumn always seems to leave us the poorer. As it is absolutely freezing today, I hope they don't turn tail and head back south prematurely. The wise old Scots had a saying "Cast nae cloot till May be oot" and given the current temperature, I don't think I'll be shedding any layers of clothing yet a while.

I now wake with the sun already high in the sky and there is still sufficient daylight to read a newspaper outside at 10.30pm. In other words, it can be a long day if you feel inclined to make maximum use of the light. What with walks morning and night, and gardening in between times, I am exhausted at the end of the day.

After visiting a neighbour's magnificent garden I am reminded once again just what can be achieved by way of horticulture at this latitude. It is an impressive sight and the season still young. There is a riotous display of daffodils and tulips while at the same time fruit has already formed on apples, apricots and a variety of berry bushes inside a huge poly-tunnel. On leaving, I am presented with a bunch of rhubarb, the stalks of which are as thick as my wrist – and this still early May! Thus inspired I return to my modest piece of ground and fancifully plan how I mean to transform it. Sea views will have to wait.

Now that the garden is dug and potatoes planted the weather has reverted to winter. Am I too early off the mark? Probably. That garden I visited yesterday was well protected by hedges and the lay of the land. By contrast, my plot is very exposed. After a couple of snowy showers sun decides to make a reappearance in the late afternoon and the cliff backdrop that dominates our view makes a curtain-call as cloud shadow is peeled away to the south. The matinee performance promises to be sparkling and animated. We have the best seats in the house. And, having said that, it's snowing again!

> *The waves beside them danced; but they*
> *Out-did the sparkling waves in glee:*

… lines from William Wordsworth's poem *Daffodils* and so very apt to the current scene around Aywick where fields of them abound on every side and the waves have little chance of competing for attention. There must be thousands of daffodils 'dancing' on the slopes above the bay, splashes of yellow sunlight sprung out of the ground to contradict the morbid skies and turn the world upside-down. Is there anything more cheerful or appealing than daffodils? They make me smile.

The configuration of the brae on which we live is such as to create an updraft off the sea, which at times translates into a thermal. It is sufficient to allow gulls to float along the hidden air current at all hours of the day and they appear to do so with great *joie de vivre*, riding back and fore effortlessly and with scarcely any perceptive movement of their wings. This scintillating aerial ballet is wonderful to watch. It smoothes ruffled feathers, relaxes the mind and calms the soul. I know of no better therapy for life's stresses.

So far this writing has made very little mention of fish and fishing, despite its singular preoccupation with the sea. With luck that may soon change as summer approaches and opportunities to head offshore come my way. Meanwhile we are already into the second month of the sea trout, salmon, and brown trout season in northern Scotland and there is nothing stopping me casting a fly in the direction of any or all of these – nothing that is except the need of rod and line. So… today I head into Lerwick to rectify the situation.

It must be all of 25 years since I last took any serious interest in the sport and prior to that, I was as liable to bore folk to death with piscatorial stories as the next occa (obsessively compulsive crazy angler). But that all changed for a variety

SEA VIEW

of reasons (none of which are relevant to this particular writing) and I disposed of all my gear: hook, line and sinker. In the interim I have forgotten most of what I knew except those evocative fly names – Jock Scott, Greenwell's Glory, Butcher, Peter Ross, Zulu… these never change and can never be forgotten. They seem destined to lure every fisherman (if not every fish) till "aa the seas gang dry". As it is, I let myself be talked into buying a packaged deal – four-piece rod, reel, tapered line and handy carrying case. A couple of spare casts and a selection of flies, the names of which are all new to me and I'm set to 'wet a line'. I still feel I'd like a Zulu and a Butcher in my fly-box, if only for their let's-be-clear-who's-in-charge-here image, but we'll see what the fish have to say to Kate McLaren, Brown Sedge and Clan Chief. At least the names sound suitably Scottish and who am I to quibble. The last time I cast a fly it was about four times as big as any of these and went by the name of Black Matuka. But that, as I say, was a long time ago and several thousand miles from here.

Back at The Horse (still no puffins), I watch a pair of wily crows as they attempt to scare fulmars off their nests in order to steal eggs. Time and again the crows dive with outstretched claws straight at the occupied cliff ledges, chased all the while by the nesting birds' anxious mates. Several times I feel sure the harassed nest-sitters will be forced to take evasive action as the crows look about to strike them head on, but every time the fulmars sit tight, meeting bluff with counter-bluff and the crows turn away thwarted yet again. One crow, thoroughly pissed off by lack of success, lands on a ledge and angrily picks up a small stone, tossing it into space with a flick of its head then peering down to watch it land in the sea far below. The action is so like that of a spoilt child I can't help laughing. Eventually the crows fly off in disgust though doubtless they'll be back. Empty eggshells on the cliff top are evidence of earlier successes. Fortune favours the brave (or the persistent) and that can be as true for crows as it is for fulmars.

If the puffins won't come to me then I will have to go to them. Though we do not set off with this in mind, we end up travelling all the way to Sumburgh lighthouse at the southern end of Shetland where, we are reliably informed, a colony of puffins arrived some weeks ago. The original plan was to spend the day visiting family on Bressay but everyone declares it is such a beautiful day we should all go and visit the puffins. It is 23 years since I last travelled the road from Lerwick to Sumburgh and I am amazed at the increased amount of housing in the region of Gulberwick, Cunningsburgh and Sandwick, especially as in the interim the overall population of the islands has remained more or less static. Further south we detour past St Ninian's Isle and the Bay of Scousbrough where we count 38 seals basking on the sand (*see photo page xi*). This is one of my favourite districts in Shetland and one which now evokes many happy memories. Today the scenery, the weather, and the company are all unsurpassable.

Sumburgh lighthouse looks in need of a facelift and a lack of adequate viewing platforms in this popular birdwatcher's paradise is strangely out of character when compared with other projects the progressive Shetland Islands Council throws money at. There are fewer puffins than we expected to find and they are all in awkward spots, difficult to photograph. Listening to comments of tourists, who appear to be a broad representation of the international community, it is apparent many of them, like me, expected to find better viewing facilities. Oh well, it is early days and this particular one is altogether too lovely to be spoiled by grumbling.[*1]

Shetland is a magnet to many varieties of sea-goers besides puffins and back in Lerwick we note the harbour is beginning to become enlivened with the arrival of sailing craft from various European countries. In the coming weeks and months this will be a busy port as all manner of vessels turn up to join the party.

I'm out good and early on a cloudless day to be rewarded with another otter encounter. This one is so nonchalantly laid-back that I could practically pat it on the head though to do so would scarcely be wise. As it is, we exchange greetings (in a manner of speaking) and go our separate ways. Don't get me wrong, I am not about to become blasé about these charismatic rascals.

The sea is shining. This is about as good as it gets. Intending to get ahead with a variety of pressing chores I end up spending much of the day engrossed in and captivated by the sea and its changing moods.

"… each day is a splendiferous spewing of sun and cool breeze, a delicious dream of islet vistas crowned with gambolling cloudlets like fleeing sheep. Isn't island life wondrous? Once an islander, always an islander…" So says my New Zealand correspondent and he might be describing life in Yell rather than Waiheke.

In a five-day stretch of magnificent weather, sea is the dominant feature. It embraces me in tranquil equanimity with no hint of malice. Passive, docile, submissive; I could easily forget this dormant creature is in reality deep and deceptive. If the Pacific was named because it is supposedly calm and peaceful by nature (something I know to be untrue), how much less should I be deceived by this azure expanse that is singing me a beguiling siren song. And yet, I am enthralled, spellbound, charmed, enchanted and a whole lot more.

Sea is calm. Light shifts across its surface changing from gleaming platinum to pewter as a bank of fog drifts indeterminately through the sound. Inshore rocks are starkly etched; deep engravings on an otherwise ill-defined print. After yesterday's sparkling animation, my world has become dumbed down. All of nature is holding its breath in expectation of some apocalyptic event. However, in the time it takes to write this the curtain falls on Act 1. Fog envelopes the land. I could change channels but the view (or lack of it) is the same on every side. It has become a case of "watch this space for further developments". By mid-afternoon sun has broken through to enliven the show's finale and a late evening walk along the coast is a memorable encore. Sea is calm.

I would like to relate the tale of the lovely three-pound brown trout that gave me a noble fight before I finally landed it on that grassy verge of the loch, or better still the riveting story of a five-pound salmon that got away. Alas, it would

---

*   I am reliably informed Shetland Amenity Trust has big plans for the Sumburgh Lighthouse and environs.

SEA VIEW

all be fantasy. Not a bite. Not a nibble. Nary so much as an alluring swirl or an enticing shadow beneath the loch's surface. Am I disappointed? Not a bit of it. Fly fishing is about being there; absorbing the tranquillity that can only be found on a loch after sunset. Some of us even find the fish are a distraction from the main game… I mean, what else can I say? Kate McLaren has tried all her wiles, tripping and dancing o'er stippled waters while stodgy old Brown Sedge has dibbled and dabbled on darkling pools. Clan Chief looks a tad too flamboyant to be trotted out this early in the season, but I could be wrong. I think it's time to head to the pub and drink in some local lore.

Rising temperatures are luring people to the seaside in Brighton and Bournemouth – quite possibly further north too, but not *this* far north. Here we are blanketed in sea fog, and calm though it may be, the air and sea are still much too cold to tempt any but the foolhardy. I may be a fool but I'm not hardy. Besides, the sea looks like a sheet of aluminium. I might dent it (or my skull) if I dive in.

And still the fog persists. It may not be conducive to lifting flagging spirits but the humidity coupled with nigh on 20 hours daylight is sure as hell making the garden happy. Talk about watching grass grow!

And now the rain gently falls. I can hear the flowers laughing. On black cliffs gulls sit tight while predators hunch their backs on other lofty eyries and await the sun.

On a fifth day of mist-cum-rain I am reminded of a favourite story. A camera-slung American tourist steps from his hire-car into the rain-swept and all-but-deserted street of a Scottish highland village. Accosting an old man out walking his dog, the visitor grumbles, "What do you do in this Gawd-forsaken place when it rains?" The old man looks him in the eye then quietly replies, "We dinna interfere." Three words only, yet such delicious understatement of a total philosophy. Not only was the local worthy succinctly implying that he did not share the view that his village was God-forsaken, but that on the contrary God was in control and His will was sacrosanct. Clearly, the intent was to deliver a gentle rebuke to someone who would do better to accept his fate than rail against it. Presumably there were things to do in a highland village on a rainy day but the tourist had forfeited his right of discovery by taking God's name in vain. Furthermore, the notion that anyone might actually be *able* to interfere in the ordering of the weather, however much he may wish to do so, is quaint to say the least.

I pass by a house where a number of model fishing boats are sitting on top of a dry-stone wall and I am reminded (as if I needed reminding) of how the sea is so much a part of everyone's life in this part of the world. The man who created these scale models in intricate detail has spent all his working life as a fisherman. Now in retirement, he paints bright pictures on flat stones or sketches in pen and ink – always boats – and in summer he places his models on top of the wall for all to see. I must return and take a photograph.

The hills are alive with the sound of seagulls. Taking a short-cut home from the seashore I pass by a hill crest where a small flock of gulls has established their

SEA VIEW

Above: **West Sandwick beach on a fine spring day.** *(See page 45)*

Below: **Author's pastel drawing of Kaywick.** *(See page 5)*

SEA VIEW

Above: **The Dale of Lumbister.** *(See page 55)*

Below: **Bressay Lighthouse.** *(See page 58)*

SEA VIEW

Above: The ever changing view from my front window. In the foreground is The Poil with Fetlar forming a backdrop across Colgrave Sound.

Below: Seals sunning themselves on Rerwick beach (South Mainland). *(See page 70)*

SEA VIEW

Above: **Puffin at The Horse of Burravoe.** *(See page 83)*

Below: **Waterfall on the Burn of Lunklet near Aith.**

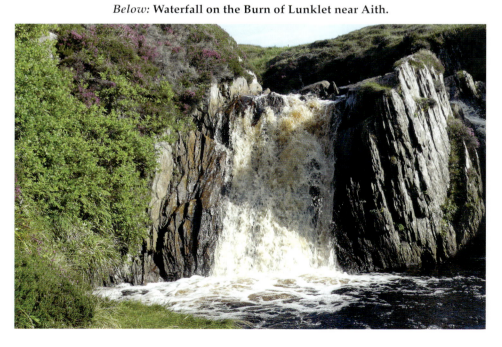

SEA VIEW

Left: **Marsh Marigold**
(Caltha palustris).

Right: **Monkey Flower**
(Mimulus guttatus).

Above: **Wild flowers at Aywick, Yell. Meadow Buttercups**
(ranunculas acris).

Left: **Yellow Iris**
(Iris pseudoacorus).

Right: **A fat lamb in a field of daisies.**

SEA VIEW

Summer sunset from behind my house.

SEA VIEW

Autumn sunrise from in front of my house.

SEA VIEW

Ready, steady, go! (*See page 75*)

nests. I detour to take a look, setting off a raucous clamour. There are perhaps 20 nests snugly lined with dry sphagnum and bits of heather. It is easy to see why people once gathered gull's eggs to eat. There are three to a nest, each about the size of a bantam's egg. I wonder if they taste at all fishy but I'm not tempted to find out. A couple of quick photos and I'm out of there. It doesn't pay to hang around when the sky is full of wheeling gulls unless you don't mind being shat upon. A little further on, in marshy ground near a loch, I come on a lapwing's nest with one egg, and at the loch side the robbed out remains of what might have been a red-throated diver's nest. Two empty shells, dark green and elongated – an otter's snack or perhaps the outcome of marauding skuas. Certainly too early for hatchlings. I hope they find another loch and better luck before the season passes.

One of the nests from yesterday's visit to the gull colony.

Spring evening

Woolly clouds graze Fetlar's distant hills. Sunlight is moulded and folded where they slope to darkling sea. Like drifting snowflakes, gulls meld out of the light into cliff shadow while beyond them on grassy knolls other drifts are the bedded lambs. In a hollow behind the house a nesting curlew turns to face the setting sun, and far off on North Sea's horizon a ship passes from sight.

SEA VIEW

A perfect day. Driving north through the island I observe several men working at cutting or raising peat. Earlier in this narrative I commented that one rarely sees any open peat banks in Shetland today. Could be I was wrong as I now count over twenty within half as many miles. Not that this constitutes any sort of return to the days when every household relied on peat for fuel but it is a significant number nonetheless and some of the men I am passing today appear to be newcomers to this comparatively skilled work. Perhaps all this talk of increasing fuel costs in the future has prompted a re-think. Whatever the reason, there is something very satisfying about a bank of newly cut peat. Money in the bank, you might say. Yell has arguably the best peat in Shetland: black, tightly compacted and almost coal-like when dried. It is a clean product to handle and burns brightly with an aromatic blue smoke that is not at all unpleasant. The residual ash is very fine, indicating the high combustibility of this excellent fuel. Too bad my house is all-electric or I might have been tempted to buy a tushkar and revisit those "good old days". Then again, it is a back-breaking business…

Where have all the wild flowers gone? Squills, ragged robin, primroses (there used to be whole fields of them), wild thyme (I recall roadsides carpeted in pink), orchids, moss campion… I could go on. True, hardy thrift continues to brighten cliff tops while marsh-marigolds and yellow iris hold sway along the ditches and swampy ground, but what of the rest? I'm told that some years ago Shetland Island Council sprayed pesticides on the road verges. Whoever was responsible for that decision ought to be tarred and feathered. Shame!

Banksflooers, sea pinks, thrift, *armeria martima*; call it what you will and I have mentioned it a time or two already. More commonly associated with the cliffs of Cornwall or Wales, Shetland is also a great place to see this hardiest of plants, which grow along the tops of cliffs and in crevasses all the way down to the sea. Folklore tells of fishermen finding their way home in dense sea fog by steering a course towards the honeyed scent of the banksflooers which is carried far offshore on the faintest breeze. Logic would tell you no flower could hope to survive on Shetland's cliffs, yet survive and thrive these amazingly resilient plants most certainly do; sending their taproots deep into any fissure to tough out the wildest weather nature can throw at them. If you wanted a logo that represented survival in adversity you could not choose better than this tenacious flower.

I suppose it is not unreasonable to expect to see otters in Otterswick but, in fact, I visit the region several times before I am rewarded. It is worth the wait. Early this morning I am passing along the top of a low cliff when the sound of a splash in the water below catches my attention. Presently an otter surfaces and I freeze on the spot until it dives again. I've now got 30 seconds to get into a better position (the average time an otter stays under water). I begin clambering down, stopping every time my quarry reappears. Presently I am lying prone; positioned on a large slab of rock directly above a tiny geo. In the clear water it is possible to see the otter gyrating and somersaulting beneath the surface. Twice it surfaces with small fish, climbing onto a rock to eat them before turning and diving once more.

This is my best otter photo so far and likely to be as good as I'll get *(see photo page xvi)*. You can even see the water dripping from its fur. I have been closer to one but paradoxically you can be too close in that you end up looking straight down on your subject and it doesn't provide the right sort of angle for good photography. A few days ago I was walking along the bank above the seashore, just below the house and at a point where a small burn runs in, when I saw an otter that was scarcely six feet from me, going up the burn. By the time I got the camera out of the bag it had gone under a fence and into some reeds; then to my surprise it turned and, leaving the burn, headed directly to where I was standing. Coming back under the fence (obviously totally oblivious of me, as it was very preoccupied with its own business and did not look up) the otter was barely four feet from me when I took my one and only photo. Otters have very sharp hearing and an acute sense of smell but not such good eyesight. Anyway, it heard the click of the camera and immediately looked up (having got the shock of its life). In a flash it bolted down a nearby rabbit burrow. The resulting photo was very disappointing. I didn't even bother keeping it on file.

And now we are discovering the ultimate benefit of living by the sea – especially *this* sea. Fish, fish, and more fish! The little boats are out. The mackerel season has begun early and there are lots more besides: ling, cod, coalfish, skate, monkfish, haddock, and scallops to name a few. Good neighbours are coming to our door with ready-filleted fish along with handy hints on the best way to cook it. "Try smearing a little mustard on the mackerel and grilling it. Add salt and pepper," advises one. Always open to advice we do exactly that. Delicious! No sooner have we enjoyed the meal than the same benefactor is back with more; this time it is lightly smoked. I can hardly wait to try it. Until a few weeks ago I had quite forgotten this marvellous fringe benefit of living in a small Shetland community. It is utopia, seventh heaven and Shangri-la all rolled into one.

Some pages back I made reference to shipping in Colgrave Sound and since then have discovered that I can learn about passing vessels at www.marine traffic. com (Live Ships Map) where movement of all shipping is tracked via satellite. As I write, the Norwegian tanker *Clipper Sky* arrives off The Poil to lie under the cliffs of Fetlar awaiting a berth at Sullom Voe Oil Terminal. The website gives me relevant information such as tonnage, length, breadth and so on. I might become a latter-day ship spotter – supposing I have nothing better to do. On my way across the headland to obtain a photograph, I come on a ringed plover's nest. It is a lucky find as they are well camouflaged. Now this is more my kind of spotting, and given the current brouhaha surrounding the massive undersea oil leak in the Gulf of Mexico, where millions of barrels of oil are escaping into the surrounding ocean and causing as yet untold damage, I think spotting oil tankers is possibly for the birds.

Returning along the cliffs from The Poil I notice a length of stout rope, one end anchored round a large rock and the other hanging down a steep slope to the sea. Nearby is an older, frayed version of the same. Both ropes give somewhat precarious access to a deep, wide-mouthed geo that doubtless receives the lion's

SEA VIEW

share of any flotsam coming this way. It is a reminder of the extent to which some people will go in order to salvage what the sea brings to our shores. Having already alluded to this before I will not elaborate further except to say "rather him than me on that rope!" So far my own beachcombing has been limited to the odd broken plank (including those bits I salvaged on Bressay) but, like a true Shetlander, I have not wasted what I have found and can now boast a couple of quite handsome if rustic 'banks rekk' flower boxes.

I've found the perfect fishing spot and not a mile from home! The loch is rather shallow but there is a deep, dark stream running into it from the peat hill behind *and* there are fish here. Later in the season I may expect to find sea trout. For the time being I must be content with what's on offer – small brown trout. I manage to entice a couple to investigate my proffered Clan Chief fly and they are definitely interested, if somewhat shy. Patience, rather than luck, is the necessary requisite of the successful fly-fisher. Without it, he may expect to go home with an empty bag more often than not. The stream is narrow and I will need to approach its banks with utmost stealth.

Having made a good reconnoitre I will return here well after sunset on another day and hope for success. Meanwhile it is a picturesque spot with lots of wildflowers carpeting the meadows to either side. A lovely place to spend an hour or two, with or without successful fishing. And, incidentally, already I am finding the observation made last week regarding Shetland's wildflowers may have been premature. There are still discoveries to be made and the season is young.

We were holidaying on Sognefjord in Norway and I had hired a rowing boat to take my Aunt Isobel out on the fjord. It was calm as a duck pond. The water was cloudy and a strange luminous green: the effect of glacial melt following unusually high temperatures over the preceding days. Water temperature, however, was close to freezing. We had a most enjoyable outing, crossing the fjord to land on a rocky outcrop from where we climbed a little knoll to admire the view. Returning to the jetty below the hotel, I contrived to bring the boat in stern first, reckoning this would create maximum stability for Aunt Isobel to climb ashore. My intention was to hold the boat in position against the pier ladder by back paddling. I failed to recognise the strong current running under the pier. I also failed to allow for my aunt's advanced age. By rights, I should have come alongside and tied up. The old lady stood in the stern facing the pier and took hold of the ladder I had so carefully manoeuvred up to. Now came the tricky bit. My sculling was out of synchronisation. We began to drift away on the current. "Let go," I called, "and I'll reposition the boat." The words fell on deaf ears. Like a drowning kitten, my aunt clung on desperately. The oars were at full stretch so had no purchase whatsoever. As the gap widened, the woman's body weight began to transfer to the pier, further exacerbating the problem. The boat was now being *pushed* away with increasing rapidity. I grappled the unwieldy oars in desperation but the moment of truth had arrived. As I finally dug deep to reverse the drift, Aunt Isobel gracefully disappearing over the stern like a seal sliding

76

SEA VIEW

off a rock. *Then* she let go of the ladder! Disappearing into the murky depths, she bobbed up like a cork a moment later. By good fortune I simultaneously completed my stroke to come alongside her and, without knowing how, snatched the enraged and spluttering woman from the water and clamped her to the ladder. That I succeeded in doing so without so much as getting my feet wet seemed to infuriate her all the more. Once safely on the pier she fixed me with a glare (doubtless made frostier by the freezing water). "You did that deliberately," she snarled through chattering teeth. Nothing could have been further from the truth but it took the best part of a bottle of Bristol Cream Sherry to convince the old dragon. By the next day, we were the best of friends once more. It is hard to believe that this episode in my life took place over forty years ago. It might have been yesterday for the clarity of the recollection.

For several days now sea has been eerily calm under leaden skies. Strange patterns are being etched on its silvery surface and the horizon is frequently indistinguishable. At times a nearer, false horizon has made distant boats appear to be floating in the sky. As is frequently the case in such weather, all of nature is oddly silent and in the absence of air movement the usual drift of gulls has vanished. Whatever the origin of the word 'doldrums', its meanings of stagnation, gloominess or a sluggish state in which energy levels are low seem to add up to a good description of what I am looking out upon at the moment. If depression had a suit of clothing this would be it and if one could choose their sea view it is unlikely any would opt for this one.

Late evening brings improvement when apricot tinted clouds cast a saffron sheen on the ocean. About a mile offshore, a school of mackerel is disturbing the surface in characteristic fashion.

Having represented yesterday as calm, I am now at a loss for a more placid word to describe this morning. Yet I would need one. From shore to horizon the sea is as glass. Standing on the beach at Salt Wick I marvel at the sight and when a seal's head breaks the surface it is as though a sacrilege has been committed. Two hours later, and against all odds, a fresh south-easterly is creating whitecaps. Little boats that have been lured out to a peaceful day's fishing are scurrying for home. And still it freshens. Clouds are sent packing (along with yesterday's black dog) and for the first time in days sea is sparkling blue. Does this mean it is going to be fine tomorrow…? No. The black dog returns to bite me in the bum. I refuse to be intimidated however and turn my back on the gloomy scene.

Inside the sheltering arm of Fetlar the sea is a sheet of aluminium foil with dark lines where it has been slightly crumpled. Further out, sun-streaked rougher water sits proud of the horizon in bands of shimmering silver. The animation could easily be a mirage though it seems to be caused by the north-easterly which is having little effect inshore. Black rocks at the southern extremity of Fetlar, known as the Horn of Ramness, are grim sentinels guarding the entrance to Colgrave Sound. This is a popular fishing ground and several small boats are out taking advantage of the sheltered conditions under Fetlar's cliffs. Catches coming ashore include ling, pollack, cod, mackerel, and what Shetlanders call piltocks (young coalfish). These are recreational fishermen and they spend almost as much time ashore cleaning, filleting and distributing their catch among neighbours as they do at sea. The old traditions of salting and smoking some of the catch are still part and parcel of the enterprise – not out of necessity but merely for the pleasurable variation of taste that results. There is nothing quite as enticing in the line of fish as a lightly smoked mackerel or haddock, especially when the whole procedure from hook to plate is completed within the space of 24 hours.

My beachcombing has taken on a life of its own and it has all to do with the garden. At least two or three times a week I shoulder a little rucksack in which I keep a trowel and some plastic bags. Aywick and Salt Wick beaches have lots of smooth round stones of all sizes and colours and I am gradually gathering a selection; some to create a rockery, others for pebble paths or various 'features'. The trowel and plastic bags are for collecting sea pinks (thrift) and one or two other hardy 'banks flooers' that are forming borders and helping add colour to my embryo garden. I also bring home bags of seaweed to fertilise what is otherwise very poor soil. If a dripping tap can wear away stone then presumably my regular trips to the beach will eventually net results that are measurable in personal satisfaction if not observable improvement on the home front.

Much of the coastline hereabouts is made up of cliffs, with the occasional rocky beach and rarer sandy one. The cliffs are for the most part sheer and awesome, rising in places to over 200ft. Almost every suitable ledge is tenanted by nesting gulls and every nook and cranny from top to bottom is festooned with clumps of wildflowers. Pink thrift predominates followed by yellow roseroot with, here and there, patches of white sea campion, blue sheep's-bit, lilac sea rocket and more. To stand anywhere near the top is to be intoxicated by the scent which wafts up on the air currents. The Hanging Gardens of Babylon might have been brighter and more diverse but I doubt if their setting was as spectacular or its residents as smugly pleased with themselves as these gulls appear to be. Though I take many photos, I am unable to replicate the scene to my satisfaction. To parody Kipling: "But the cliff it is large and man he is small. Let him think and be still."

And still the days are grey. Grey sea on which greyer boats drift past greyest cliffs. I need a diversion. I wonder if the fish are biting. Only one way to find out. On the way to my chosen stream I cross a mossy field full of orchids. There must be tens of thousands. They are the heath spotted orchid (*dactylorhiza maculata*) and are shaded from pale pink to cerise. And here was me thinking the wildflowers had all disappeared! No magic carpet could bring more delight. There is a light breeze rippling the surface of the narrow stream. Medium cloud cover. It looks promising. I fancy my chances with 'Clan Chief'. Very soon I am being encouraged by nibbles though the trout are obviously small. It takes half an hour before I eventually hook one. Yes, it is small. The generally accepted size limit is ten inches and this one just makes nine-and-a-half. Being my first for the season I decide to keep it. Three tiddlers go back however. I've seen bigger sardines. Ah well, it's a start.

SEA VIEW

Bits of fluff seen on the hill today: bog cotton (*eriophorium vaginatum*) and chicks of the common gull (*larus canus*). The first like ballerinas, jauntily showing off for all to see; the others hoping that by hiding their heads they have rendered their fat bums invisible.

Charlie telephones from Lerwick to tell us the first yachts in the Shetland Round Britain and Ireland Race are arriving in Lerwick and we ought to be able to see some of the others as they pass outside of Fetlar. Sure enough, late in the day when the sky clears ahead of a fresh northerly, we sit in our eyrie with spy-glasses trained on the open sea and watch some of the action. Brightly coloured spinnakers backed by gleaming white mainsails. They pass quickly through our field of vision adding a touch of excitement to an otherwise ordinary day.

Tomorrow the Bergen to Lerwick race gets under way and more yachts will be heading our way. Our armchair sea view usually consists of fishing boats, occasional freighters and tankers. This livelier action is a welcome change. If it were not that I have other things to attend to, I'd be tempted to head for Lerwick where the coming weekend promises to be an exciting one. Looks like I'll have to be content to view the action on the Lerwick harbour webcam. A poor substitute but better than nothing.

Returning to Breckon today I stand in the nearby burial ground listening to the wind and waves and it seems to me there are few places anywhere in the world that are more beautiful. A short while ago we laid a loved one to rest here. Now the grave is covered with flowers. Others stand beside me, heads bowed. No one speaks. All are listening. A requiem is being sung. It is the eternal requiem of wind and waves.

This morning at 9am, Adaline and I board the ferry *Daggri* at Ulsta (Yell) to go on what has been billed as a Midsummer Cruise. It is overcast and the sea is lumpy. It does not bode well but we have paid for our tickets so... The original plan was to round the top of Shetland's mainland and visit some of the more spectacular cliffs and stacks in that region. After taking on the rest of our passengers at Toft (Shetland mainland), we head north through Yell Sound on the understanding that if the sea is too rough beyond Fethaland, we will alter

SEA VIEW

course and cross to the relative shelter of Yell's west coast. In essence, this is what transpires although we manage to get close to the jagged teeth of Ramna Stacks first.

Looking at camera equipment in the hands of several other passengers (some of it rivals the aforementioned stacks) I am almost too embarrassed to bring my 12 mega-pixel midget out of its bag. Then again, with the ferry pitching and rolling in this swell, it is no place for handheld photography when the barrel lenses are half a metre long. Pretending indifference, I obtain some passable photographs in the cloudy conditions and wonder if the pros have done any better.

After completing a rectangular course that takes in all of Yell Sound, we continue round the southern extremity of Yell before steering north once more to enter Colgrave Sound. There are blinks of sunshine now and the sea is much calmer. This is home territory although to date I have only viewed it from shore. Looking at the cliffs from a seaward perspective I find they appear less dramatic and less menacing than when viewed from the top. From here, they are still wild and dangerous beasts but their claws are concealed. The Horse of Burravoe looks positively benign and it occurs to me that many of these cliffs have been named by seamen who view them principally as landmarks on which to take their bearings rather than the treacherous hazards to shipping that they surely are.

Our cruise continues northwards as far as Gutcher before crossing the sound to return along Fetlar's rugged coastline. By now, the sea is a veritable millpond making for ideal conditions in which to sight dolphins and whales. Alerted to this possibility it is not long before someone spots a minke whale and our skipper obligingly alters course to bring us closer. All the long lenses are now bristling like guns to port and starboard (Nelson's *Victory* could scarcely have looked more menacing) though it is doubtful anyone manages to obtain a worthwhile photograph as the whale is decidedly camera-shy and the light is by no means perfect. No one appears to be unduly disappointed as everyone is thoroughly enjoying themselves, making new friends or reacquainting with old ones. It is 5.30pm when we berth at Toft and the first of the passengers reluctantly go ashore. Half an hour later we are back on the road to Aywick. What started out as a rough passage ends in unbelievably calm seas. Forecast rain never materialised and, just when we needed it most, sun broke from cloud to illuminate the more dramatic stretches of cliff scenery. As sea views go, today's was definitely among the best.

This being the longest day, sun is above the horizon for 19 hours at 60° 33.5' north – or in other words where I live – and during the remaining five hours it passes beneath the most northerly rim providing perpetual twilight which in Shetland is referred to as the "simmer dim". In all, the sun's path executes an ellipse that takes in practically the entire compass, rising at about the 50 degrees point and setting at 310 degrees. For those unfamiliar with the compass this equates with rising at approximately the '2' position on a watch face and setting at '10' which, incidentally, is near enough to the actual hours of sunrise and sunset in midsummer.

SEA VIEW

On the midsummer cruise two days ago our ferry came to within half a mile of cliffs at a spot named Kistrif, near Burravoe in South Yell, from where I could clearly see a colony of guillemots on a sloping ledge 50 feet or so above sea level. At the time, a fellow passenger claimed to have seen a puffin in flight near the boat. Being virtually adjacent to the Horse of Burravoe, it occurs to me that this may be where the puffin colony is rather than at the Horse. Today being fine and calm I decide to check out my supposition. The cliff in question is within half a mile of the Burravoe marina so I reach it in a matter of minutes after parking the car. Sure enough, besides the guillemots, I find several puffins high up on the cliff face. The area is fenced off for safety reasons and none of the burrows are within range of my camera. Nevertheless, I am delighted to have at last established contact with these elusive little birds and will return on a brighter day in hope of finding a suitable angle for photography. For the time being it is enough just to know they are here and I enjoy viewing them through the binoculars. Nearby I come upon a black guillemot or tystie as they are locally known. It is standing on a low, grassy ledge at no great distance from me and appears untroubled by my proximity. I manage to obtain several good photographs before moving on. Next on the scene is a fulmar that is sitting under an overhanging bank less than a couple of feet above the beach. This bird is likewise unperturbed by my presence though I am not so foolish as to go too close. Nesting fulmars can regurgitate and squirt a disgusting vomit on anyone who makes the mistake of overstepping the mark. I'm content to let the camera's zoom do the close-up bit. There is a colony of arctic terns (tirricks) nearby. These too are deserving of a wide berth and are quick to warn me accordingly, diving in anger long before I am anywhere near their precious nests. From a bird-watching point of view it has been a very satisfactory morning.

Today's little irony is that sea fog has effectively obliterated my sea view. I can scarcely see across the road. It is a state of play that holds throughout the day and therefore any observation I might make is inevitably going to be the product of a clouded mind or, as Paul might phrase it: *through a glass, darkly*. A day for introspection or reflection…

other music,
like the creak of oars
or the tremble of taut rigging;
whispered god-voices carried on wind
and murmured in streams soon to enter sea's embrace;
waves booming in deep caverns
where bird-cries echo –
and echo
while tides attend far off shores,
bringing faded messages
which other tides turn
and turn again;

SEA VIEW

singing in crested surf
or chuckling in pebbles
until the last to hear are the ebb-crabs
whose sibilant voices
not even the timeless sand can know.

It is the sailing season yet yachts lie idle at their moorings. Sea has lain calm for the best part of a month now. If it were colder I might be persuaded to believe the surface was frozen. Leaden skies are beginning to weigh heavily on my mind. And already the world is tipping back on its axis. These observations and thoughts I can make from behind my desk – the view through glass is enough to trigger them. But what if I step outside, walk down through the fields and dip a hand in the ocean? No time like the present in which to find out...

Fields which a few weeks ago were close-cropped by sheep and lambs have now been closed up to make hay. Already, in what seems a matter of days, a transformation has taken place. Grass is almost up to my knees in places and the fields are full of wildflowers. I say hay, but in reality it is likely to be silage which is generally reckoned to be more nutritious and in this climate hay-making can be a convoluted and chancy business. Walking on down through almost eerie silence (no bleating lambs, no strident bird calls) I reach the sea. Low tide. Crystal clear rock pools invite closer inspection. It is a child's wonderland. Sea is indeed calm but it is not still. It heaves restlessly under a tireless tide that having gone out has now changed its mind and is coming back in. Sea can only sigh and mutter under its breath. I collect a few more pebbles for the garden and another bag of seaweed. Tomorrow I will come again. There will be something new for me to see.

Make a definitive sort of statement one day and you can bet your bottom dollar something will come along tomorrow to contradict it. Yesterday I observed a lack of yachts this summer owing to the calm conditions, and what happens today? They turn out in force! Not because there is any wind. There is none. Sea remains like a millpond. But it's Saturday and if the local club fail to take to the water soon the season will be over. And so here they all are, sitting like ducks on said millpond. Going nowhere. Stealing no one's wind and certainly not jockeying for position. Staring at their own reflections. A pretty enough picture I dare say, but a yacht race it ain't!

It is early evening before the weather invites me out. Wind is south-easterly and freshening. Sun looks as if it is about to break free of the gossamer net that has enmeshed it all day. I set out on my favourite coastal walk – clockwise round the Ness of Queyon. Although there is fog out to sea, visibility is otherwise good. Reaching the White Wife at Otterswick I turn my back to the sea and head in a northerly direction for home. It is then, while preoccupied with climbing the grassy slope leading to open moorland, that I am unexpectedly overtaken by thick fog. At first, I think little of it. I know this area well, featureless though it is. Five minutes later, I am having second thoughts. Visibility is down to fifty yards. I am put in mind of a scene described by Catherine Marshall in her book

SEA VIEW

titled *A Man called Peter* (a scene director Henry Coster exploits to the full when making his film of the story). Peter Marshall is out walking his dog when, like me, he is surrounded by fog. He almost walks over the edge of a deep quarry. It proves to be a cathartic moment in his life. To the best of my knowledge there are no quarries here although there are some nasty drops over disused peat banks. Not that I am in any sort of danger. The fog isn't *that* thick. It is thick enough to disorientate me, however, and were it not for the cold south-easterly at my back I could easily become lost. As it is, I let the wind steer me and keeping to the high ground I continue more or less north in the expectation of eventually coming upon the village. All's well that ends well. A house looms out of the fog and I know where I am. It is not where I *expected* to be however. I have deviated from my supposed path by over 300 yards. It is a sobering reminder of how easily one can become lost in this sort of terrain when fog or darkness descends. For the record, I *always* carry a compass, although that only works if you have an inkling of where you are when you start using it!

On a day of brighter weather, I get the chance to go off fishing with Peter. His boat is called *Galilean*. Does this mean he holds the keys to heaven's gate? Being in no hurry for heaven, I'll settle for a fish supper which, after all, is heaven of a sort. We leave the Mid Yell marina at about 2pm in a freshening breeze and head south down Colgrave Sound towards Ay Wick, stopping from time to time on various fishing grounds known to the helmsman. "We should get mackerel here," he says. And we do. "Piltocks (coalfish) here." And, again, he is right. In particular I watch the way Peter takes cross bearings off landmarks (Shetlanders call them meids) in order to locate these fishing grounds. Meids were important aids to navigation in olden days (they still are to some degree) and were part of the lore handed down from father to son.

In a little over an hour we catch a hundredweight of fish – 50/50 mackerel and piltocks – by which time the sea has become quite choppy and it is starting to rain. Well satisfied we head back to the moorings. It is my first such outing in more years than I care to remember. I hope for more. Meanwhile, I am about to enjoy 'catch of the day' with the promise of smoked mackerel tomorrow – courtesy of Pete, of course. With my fish supper assured I'm back to wondering about this guy's curriculum vitae.

At long last my quest to photograph puffins is rewarded *(see photo page xii)*. I've known where to find them for over a week but awaiting suitable weather has tested my patience. Today's conditions are ideal and I arrive at the Burravoe cliffs good and early, hoping for success. What I had taken to be a very small colony of perhaps no more than a dozen breeding pairs appears to be much larger. Everywhere I look there are puffins popping in and out of their burrows or standing guard on nearby rock ledges. Like the fulmars, they are not unduly alarmed by human proximity, probably because they know they are perfectly safe. Unless I was to take up abseiling I could hardly constitute a threat. Thus by judiciously exploiting the angles and the camera's 12x magnification I am able to obtain some passably good photographs. Is that astonishing beak for real! And

SEA VIEW

how about those 'clown' eyes? Shetlanders call these comical little birds 'tammy nories' though no one seems very sure exactly why. For my part, I reckon the name fits them to a T.

Standing stones and outstanding cliffs: I have returned to Unst and to a spot I visited some months ago. After photographing the Standing Stone of Bordastubble, which is reputed to be Shetland's largest, I park beside the old ruined kirk at Lund and hike up the Blue Mull. This headland guards the entrance to Bluemull Sound across from which lies the village of Cullivoe where I was born. As The Mull is over 100ft high and the sound is scarcely half a mile wide this cliff is likely to be one of the first things I clapped eyes on when I began to take an interest in my surroundings. And now here I am, 70 years later, sitting on the top and looking back in more ways than one. At the highest point the cliffs are practically sheer with very little by way of suitable ledges on which birds can nest. Consequently, there is an absence of screaming gulls and the place is unusually quiet. My focus quickly moves out to sea. Far below a roost is churning and seething and further north several holms, baas and reefs show their teeth in snarling reminder that this can be a dangerous place in a storm. And, as if that was not enough, the Bluemull Sound runs a seven-knot tide race. Nearby, at the point of the Mull, several small mounds are thought to be the remains of a monastic site. What a wild place in which to establish a religious community. And yet on a day such as this it is a place of exquisite peace and one in which a man might easily find his god.

On a bright and breezy day, I set out for town. Lerwick's seafront is a forest of masts. Yachts from a number of different countries are moored in and around the Small Boat Harbour, their flags, sails and draped anoraks making a colourful spectacle. At this time of year many foreign tongues can be heard along the street, especially Norwegian, Faroese, Dutch and German, although when one includes crew from tankers and other freighters the mix is truly international.

In an increasingly overcrowded world an ultimate irony is to be found in the way in which people in remote areas struggle to survive due to depopulation. In particular many small islands that once held thriving communities now face desertion as last survivors prepare to pack their bags and move to the 'big smoke'. Yet, in the midst of this decolonisation, there is a paradox. Many city dwellers yearn for space and dream of escaping to those very islands that others are clamouring to leave.

In reality, modern-day communication ensures no man is an island nor can he hope to escape simply by seeking isolation. The sea charts that once made some parts of the world seem as inaccessible as outer-space no longer bear those daunting "here be dragons" warnings and in any case we now have wings and can fly where we please. Strange, then, that the lemming-like rush to high-rise existence continues apace. Is it simply a case of ignorance? Do those citified dreamers secretly fear the loneliness of island life while islanders long for the city lights? Or is it that everyone's Shangri-la is on the other side of the fence?

SEA VIEW

Where wind and tide are like-minded, 'lanes' form on the surface of the sea. These are especially apparent under today's relatively calm conditions and when viewed from my elevated spot. Doubtless, there is a more scientific explanation for this phenomenon, but, as it is not readily to hand and as I much prefer to sit and enjoy the subtle changes that are constantly taking place before me, you will have to do your own research. These 'lanes' as I have termed them, which are always smoother than the surrounding sea, are sometimes wide roads and sometimes narrow paths that run out from the shore in more or less parallel duplication. They appear and disappear, expanding and contracting in inexplicable fashion before my eyes. Is there anything so animated as the surface of the sea or anyone so delighted by it as I am? And in this particular corner there are several areas which are popular with local fishermen, so on a fine day like today there is always the added attraction of little boats arriving out of the blue. Or I might lift my eyes to the horizon and see the merchantmen go by. Large freighters following sea-lanes of another sort as they ply their trade to far-off ports with strange sounding names like Reykjavik and Vladivostok. It reminds me of that poem we learned at school… "Where are you going to all you big steamers?".

I board the Yell Sound ferry *Daggri* at 10.30am en route to Lerwick. Half a mile out the throb of the engine changes and we begin to lose way. Curious, I leave the car and go up to the lounge. Directly ahead of us a pod of orcas (killer whales) is circling a shoal of fish. This is a commuter ferry with a schedule to keep, but this is also Shetland where, I'm happy to say, at least some of our ferry skippers have the good sense to recognise a rare opportunity for their passengers to experience something special and so, for the next fifteen minutes, we are treated to a show, the like of which most people only get to see on one of Richard Attenborough's TV spectaculars. At times there are as many as seven whales on the surface at once, twisting and turning in a feeding frenzy that has attracted a flock of gulls hoping for a piece of the action in the form of scraps. Arriving late for my appointment in Lerwick I explain the reason, earning an indulgent smile and a shrug. For centuries, Shetlanders have learned to accommodate the vagaries of weather and tide. A few minutes lost in admiration of orcas are neither here nor there.

There is a law of averages – I'll call it Christie's Law for want of a better name – which states that if you go walking in the hills often enough you will eventually happen upon a bird's nest. If you are really lucky it will be a skylark's and your best chance is on a windy day like today when the hen will be sitting tight and fail to hear you coming until the last second. I am telling you this because it happened to me, once, long ago. I almost stepped on a skylark's nest. Finding that tiny cup shape deep in the heather with its four exquisite sky-blue eggs was like finding a crock of gold at the end of a rainbow. I fancy my chances today and set off to climb the Ward of Otterswick, a 670-foot hill about a mile-and-a-half from the head of Otterswick. There is partial cloud cover and near gale force wind but it is not cold. I have walked many of the valleys and hills of Yell by now but this region has the most extensive erosion I have come across so far. Besides the gullies and streams there are deep sinkholes where the moor has subsided and in one of these I find the skeleton of an unfortunate sheep that has fallen in and become trapped. An ugly way to die. This would be a nasty place in winter, especially after snow has fallen. Meanwhile, though, a variety of birds including golden plovers, lapwings, snipe and oyster catchers inform me, in no uncertain terms, that I am encroaching on their territory; I fail to invoke Christie's Law. Then suddenly, as I near the crest of the Ward, I am attacked by two pairs of bonxies (great skuas) and get an inkling of what it might have been like to be a merchant seaman in one of those ill-fated Russian convoys during the war, when low-flying Stukkas and JU88s came skimming over the surface of the sea with deadly intent. I had quite forgotten how menacing bonxies can be, although I don't recall them ever coming in so low. Perhaps the strong wind is forcing them to attack at heather height. Their tactics are all the more alarming because they approach from under the brow of the hill and are upon me in a trice. Definitely below the belt. There is only one thing to do. Get the hell out of here! And there is no such thing as a dignified retreat. So I make an undignified one. Bloody bonxies!

In another season you could be forgiven for thinking this is melting snow. It isn't. It is wool. Shetland sheep have a tendency to shed their fleece in early summer, especially after an exceptionally harsh winter such as we have just had. This comes about as a result of a break in growth during the colder days, after which the old fleece separates from the new. At the beginning of last century, when times were tough, women and children would be out on the moor in summer with a bag slung across their shoulders to collect this cast off wool. It would hardly be considered a viable proposition today with premium quality

SEA VIEW

fleece fetching as little as £2 per kilo. A better choice would be to go in search of whelks or mussels in the ebb. Weight for weight you may expect to collect them in a fraction of the time and they are probably worth at least double the price.

Events have overtaken me and for the first time since commencing this writing I am playing catch-up with daily entries. It is three days since I was dodging those bonxies on the Ward of Otterswick and in the interim a local wedding has intervened to obliterate all thought of sea views from my mind. Shetland weddings are like no other. The whole community tends to become involved and the show lasts a couple of days at least. After the marriage ceremony and traditional meal comes two nights of dancing that go on into the wee small hours. It's a poor show that has you home before the rest of the world is rising to go to work. Traditional Shetland accordion and fiddle music accompanies traditional Scottish reels, which are generally notched up a gear or two as the night goes on. Sometime around midnight a supper is served to the crowded hall. The coordination required to make this happen has to be seen to be believed. Chairs are brought in so that everyone can be seated and an army of volunteers distributes tea, sandwiches and fancy cakes in copious quantity. Then, as quickly as it all appeared, the trappings are whisked away and another dance is called. Between times, at hourly intervals or thereabouts, drinks are passed round (a round of drink, in other words), though never to the point of excess… well, maybe in some cases…

As music and dancing are second nature to Shetlanders, a village wedding is always the perfect excuse to indulge in both for as long as the last man is able to remain upright – which in this case is at 6am on the second night, when someone arrives with lobsters to be cooked in the hall kitchen for the survivors! And no, I cannot claim to be one of the survivors though I gather there were enough of them to make short shrift of the lobsters.

Having briefly described a traditional Shetland wedding, it must be said this may soon be a thing of the past. Aside from the fact that fewer couples are choosing to marry, and simply opting to co-habit, many of those who decide to 'tie the knot' prefer to do so in some exotic location in company with immediate family and a handful of friends rather than having to face the nigh on impossible task of deciding who *not* to invite. Safety regulations mean that it is no longer permissible to cram the entire village into the local hall. People are offended if they are left off the list and so it has become a thankless task trying to sort out who is to receive an invitation. How easily customs and traditions become eroded when regulations are imposed.

I'm out early but not before a couple of industrious souls who are taking advantage of a fine day to get on with their peat cutting. As previously mentioned, this is something of a dying art. The Shetland method involves cutting vertically from a bank that looks like one side of a deep ditch. But before this can begin the top layer of turf must be removed. This is done with a spade, the slabs being carefully placed over the scar of the previous year's cut, thus maintaining the moor in its natural state – albeit at a lower level.

The peat-cutting tool is called a 'tushkar'. It is somewhat like a thick-handled hoe, with a broad, flat section at the end from which a forged steel blade of similar width projects downward like a narrow spade. On one or other side of the blade (depending on whether you are right or left-handed) a thin 'feather' of sharpened steel about 10 inches long juts out at right angles. Standing on top of the bank and facing along the cutting edge, the peat-cutter thrusts the tushkar downwards at a slight angle to remove a rectangular section of peat which is more or less brick-shaped though broader and flatter. The art of cutting and lifting this wet material (which must be balanced edge-on along the wide section of the handle before lifting on to the top of the bank) requires some practice. As the peats are cut downwards to two or three levels, and as many as six wide, the resulting wall formed on the top of the bank may be as much as two feet high. A skilled cutter will off-set each slab to allow wind to flow through the gaps thus aiding the drying process. The last layer is laid out on the lower side on top of the newly cut turf.

Good quality peat is dark brown to black and has very little root fibre in it. When newly cut it is similar in consistency to heavy clay without having that substance's stickiness. As it begins to dry over several days, it forms a hard crust after which the individual pieces can be lifted off the wall and set up against one another in little cones for further drying. This 'raising' is a truly back-breaking task which must be repeated after a week or two when the peats are turned over to expose the underside to wind and sun. In a wet season it may be many weeks before one's winter fuel is dry enough to cart home.

Note the first, short sections of turf under which are two longer levels that have been cut at an acute angle to facilitate lifting which is enacted in a single flowing movement. At the right hand side of the picture some of the 'wall' has already been removed and 'raised' in little cones to hasten the drying process.

A newly cut peat bank.

SEA VIEW

In bright, warm sunshine I ask my neighbour if we might now call this "summer". His answer is, "Yes, but probably only for two or three hours."

Being naturally of a more optimistic nature I determine on at least five or six. I'll let you know the outcome…

Summer, it is not! Thank goodness the library van has arrived and I can replenish my stock of reading material. For me, stepping into this literary bounty right outside my front door is akin to being a child in an ice-cream parlour. So many choices and so little time before it all melts away. I am ever conscious that my indecision is delaying the driver/librarian who has a schedule to keep – not that she gives the slightest hint of it. Permitted up to twelve books for the month, in my haste I can still generally be sure of getting at least half a dozen that I will thoroughly enjoy. Amongst today's random selection is one chosen for the title alone: *Sea Change – The Summer Voyage from East to West Scotland of the Anassa* by Mairi Hedderwick (Cannongate, 1999). With no knowledge of the author's previous work and no time to scan the back cover blurb it is very much a case of choosing a pig in a poke. Happily this one brings home my bacon in the nicest possible way. I am emotionally transported on an evocative journey to some of the most beautiful places in Scotland – places I visited 30 years ago and have forever wanted to return to. And, as if the account of that idyllic voyage is not sufficient, Mairi Hedderwick illustrates her book with exquisite watercolours to prove she is well and truly multi-talented. If my other choices fail to please I will have no hesitation in reading this one again.

Cloud shadow is racing over the sea from Fetlar changing blue-grey to navy in passing. I could probably time the speed at which it crosses the sound and thereby calculate wind velocity. I'd rather watch its lacy patterns stealing down the slopes of Stoal. Gossamer shawls being trailed one after another in idle whimsy by Queen Cassiopeia, the vain mother of Andromeda, whose boast that she was more beautiful than the sea nymph daughters of Poseidon resulted in her being tied to a chair and placed among the stars. (See how easily, on such a day, my mind turns to fantasy!) Suddenly a brightly painted red and white ship heaves into sight and I am reaching for the binoculars to try to identify it. With the aid of 'Live Ships' I learn that it is *Gerda Saele*, a Norwegian freighter bound for home. In the meantime, cloud cover increases, obliterating Cassiopeia's trivial pursuits. And another day wears to a close.

Day dawns behind lashing rain that obliterates everything except the diffused light. It is like trying to view the world from behind a waterfall. By noon it has all changed. The rainstorm has departed leaving a muslin curtain draped over the landscape. Then, within the hour, this too changes. Sea is restored into my line of vision and I return from suspended anonymity into three-dimensional normality – blue sky above a world put to rights. Island life is like no other in the way in which we appear to be cut adrift at times, floating away into uncharted seas one moment then plucked back and anchored securely where we belong; every rock a reassuring symbol of solidarity and that familiar curve of white stones and sand that constitutes 'our beach', a warm enfolding arm.

Out for my constitutional I walk inland for a change, not least because it is very blustery along the coast. At the village boundary I pause to watch one of the few remaining communal enterprises – the annual sheep shearing. There is no shearing shed you understand; this is an open air job in makeshift pens. Once upon a time not so long ago it would have involved the entire community including women and children. The fleece would have been removed by plucking or 'rooing' and the work would have taken the best part of a day. Now, with the aid of electric shears driven by portable generators, the job can be done by a few men in a couple of hours. Many of these sheep are the diminutive Shetland breed and much of their wool has long since been rubbed off on clumps of heather out on the hill. I watch what remains of a fleece being sheared from one of the flock. The job takes less than a minute and the resultant wool is little more a handful. Its weight would scarcely exceed 300gms. At £2 per kilo for premium grade it is patently obvious that there is no money in this business. So why do it? Well, first and foremost this is not about wool growing per se. All these men have other jobs. Turning out on their day off to shear a handful of pitifully small sheep is a waste of time. In fact, one man tells me that last year he dumped his wool clip as the freight to Lerwick would have cost more than it was worth. Owning sheep on what is known as the scattald (common hill grazing) means that a man owns or is the tenant of a croft. This in turn means he qualifies for certain subsidies and entitlements under the terms of The Crofters Commission and/or European Union (EU) regulations. There is also the added attraction of being able to negative gear other income for tax purposes. The wool may be of little value but, nevertheless, having a few sheep in the hill *can* be profitable in other ways. And then there is reestit mutton. No, not roasted (although that's good too). Reestit: salted and smoke-cured. Definitely an acquired taste and definitely not to mine but highly regarded in Shetland for all that. Having your own sheep is a desirable first step towards this product which in past centuries was a staple of the winter diet and is still enjoyed by many Shetlanders today. Modern-day crofters also have cross-breed sheep which are raised primarily for the fat lamb market but that is another story and happily a more profitable one.

On a Sunday drive we come upon a rabbit sitting at the side of the road with a mouthful of brown sheep's wool. I am able to stop the car directly adjacent to the timid little creature and take this photograph…

SEA VIEW

It looks like a bearded illustration of a Beatrix Potter character – perhaps Benjamin Bunny's grandfather. When I attempt to move for a better angle the rabbit runs off, although it does not discard what it has collected and I watch until it disappears in the hill. I can only assume this wool has been gathered to line a birthing room in a doe's burrow. Apparently rabbits have more intelligence than I previously thought.

This is the mackerel season and in the relatively calm conditions that currently prevail I can see large schools of them churning the sea's surface. The resulting choppy appearance is presumably what gave rise to the term "a mackerel sea". Now, if I could just lay my hands on a boat I might fetch us a supper.

It seems only yesterday that I was planting potatoes and already there are signs of harvest in the fields. The first hay has been cut and most of the sheep are shorn. Fat lambs will soon be going to market and fledglings are trying their wings. Those wild flowers just get better and on a day of sparkling blue sea all nature seems to be singing.

My great-grandfather, Tore Bjornson, was a Norwegian seaman, a whaler in fact. After losing his young wife and baby daughter to scarlet fever, he left his only son in care of the boy's Scottish grandparents in Tayport, Scotland, and sailed for America. He never came back, dying a recluse in a remote settlement in County Mendocino, California. In his declining years, he exchanged several letters with his son – now a Church of Scotland minister in Gartmore, Scotland – but without so much as a photo to comfort him, the young man knew virtually nothing of his father. In America, Bjornson changed his name to Johnson, thus adding substance to the doggerel that was doing the rounds of the timber camps at that time.

> *What was your name in the States?*
> *Was it Thompson or Johnson or Bates?*
> *Did you murder your wife and run for your life?*
> *Say, what was your name in the States?*

Bjornson (or Johnson as he now was) earned the nickname *Tanbark Johnson* owing to his skill in stripping wattle bark for the burgeoning tanning industry.

It was to take two more generations before anyone managed to connect the tenuous links with Norway and discover distant cousins there. In one of those quirks of human behaviour (doubtless prompted by my romantic tales about his great-great grandfather) my youngest son, Magnus, has changed his surname to Bjornson, naming *his* son Ethan Magnus. I like to think Tore Bjornson would be pleased to know that his great-great-great grandson, Ethan Magnus Bjornson, has had this book dedicated to him.

In this summer-come-lately there is so much catching up to do, I am rising at 5.30am and calling it a day at midnight. Sleep deprivation ought to be inevitable but it isn't. I am banking on recharging my batteries when the nights begin to lengthen. Plenty of time for hibernation when the crops are harvested.

SEA VIEW

Andrew, who is now in his nineties, tells me of his first experience in a sixareen when he was a boy of twelve. Wanting to accompany the men he is told by his father, who is one of the crew, that there is no room on board. Another man immediately protests that they must *make* room, saying, "I've never turned away a boy who wants to go to sea." (In his time, Andrew goes on to become commodore of the Texaco oil fleet.) Describing that first trip to the fishing grounds Andrew speaks of the nonchalant way in which the crew went about their business and their uncanny sense of direction in finding the way home when dense fog overtook them. We discuss the art of navigation in general, from sextants to modern electronic aids like GPS, which in turn reminds me of a comment I read recently which was written by a global traveller: "The fanciest kit is still only an *aid* to navigation." In discussing it now with Andrew, we are left wondering at the inherent skills of those old sailors who understood the set of the waves and seemed able to detect clues in all manner of things that would be invisible to a landlubber. In particular, I recall reading of how centuries before the use of compasses and sextants, Polynesian and Melanesian seamen navigated the Pacific Rim using only stars, flight-paths of birds and ocean currents to make accurate landfall hundreds of miles from their starting point – and this in dugout canoes! We agree that the art of reading nature's signposts is a gift that is rarely found these days. Just as good bush trackers are as scarce as hen's teeth, so seamen who can steer a course by the seat of their pants seem now to have become the stuff of legend.

Another long day. With guests wanting to see the sights we island hop to Unst where there is so much on offer by way of dramatic cliff scenery, archaeology, wildlife and history. It is a job to fit it all in. On Saxavord we hike to the most northerly point of the ness. Crossing the hillside, we encounter upward of 50 pairs of bonxies and their fully fledged offspring. While the adults circle and dive (at times too close for comfort) many of the younger birds appear to have not yet developed a sense of what might constitute danger and allow us to approach within a few yards before taking flight. Had we visited this region a couple of months earlier we would, undoubtedly, have been viciously attacked, as bonxies are amongst the fiercest defenders of breeding ground and nests. As it is, we are allowed to enjoy the experience with only the occasional shout of, "Look out, bandits at two-o'clock!"

It is a novelty to find myself reporting consecutive days of fine weather. It won't last. Our visitors are treated to a first glimpse of an otter, which together with a number of other 'firsts' is rapidly making their Shetland holiday incomparable. Will they begin to view the sea as I do and become enchanted by its moods, its siren songs and its beauty? Will they, like so many other visitors to these shores, be forever bound to return again and again?

I told you it wouldn't last! Heavy rain overnight continues well into the day before turning to foggy drizzle. Fields of cut hay will be spoiled. Nothing is assured in this land of unseasonable weather changes. By late afternoon, the sun has made a break-through. All will be forgiven and forgotten by tomorrow. Meanwhile the little boats return at day's end. It is the Mid Yell fishing competition. Time for the weigh-in. Time for the booze-up. Fishing competitions are not only about fish.

Still preoccupied with entertaining our guests we go west to multiple voe-vistas on a day of sunshine. Sullom, Brae, Voe, Walls; then on out to beautiful Dale of Walls with its view across the Atlantic to where the isle of Foula lies in misty, mystical isolation at the edge of the world. I used to come here as a child to help raise peats on the nearby hillside. The view is one that frequently appears in Shetland calendars. It is a place with many special memories including an idyllic weekend of glorious weather in the 1970s when I camped here with a scout patrol.

Our return journey is via detours to Clousta and Vementry where wild seas have eroded the coast and opened up rugged, ragged inlets above which lonely croft houses are noosted against the worst that weather can throw at them. With sparkling water and blue skies, it is easy to fall under the spell of these picturesque, peaceful hideaways and forget how harshly wind and sea will beset them in winter, laying siege to all and sundry.

And still those calm seas prevail. Shetland is turning on its irresistible charm. While sun continues to smile upon us we determine to make the most of it and set off for Fetlar which is the island we look across to from our home. It is often referred to as "the garden of Shetland" even though this title probably harks back to another century when the population was over 700 and the fertile soil was put to good use. Today, with scarcely 50 people on the island, there is very little cultivation and less than a dozen gardens worthy of note. To the casual observer it seems that Fetlar's future is far from assured and, despite the island's reputation as a bird watcher's paradise, it is going to take more than the remote chance of sighting a snowy owl to keep the place alive. Like Foula, Papa Stour, and Out Skerries, this is an island that seems destined to eventually become uninhabited though which will be first to gain the dubious distinction is anyone's guess. For the time being and notwithstanding the convoluted business of getting to and from the place via multiple ferry trips, it is still a picture-postcard island.

According to Laureen, they are having a heat wave in Lerwick – a heat wave hounded by midges! No such problems here. Heavy sea-fog is keeping temperature in the low teens. Our midges are mortified (would that they were petrified!). We collect stones from the beach and make more garden paths. With seaweed fertilising the soil, sea pinks lining the borders, beach stones and shells decorating layout, and driftwood planters along the wall, this has become a typical seaside garden. Ironically, it is proximity to the sea and its co-destroyer the wind that is going to be the biggest challenge when it comes to getting the garden to bloom.

It is 'Fiddle Frenzy' week in Shetland, an event which brings many fiddle players and wannabes to the island for workshops and concerts. With its long tradition of excellence in this art, Shetland never fails to host a first rate show and any of the several concerts held during the week are guaranteed to delight audiences. The nearby village of Cullivoe is renowned for its fiddle players and for always staging one of the best concerts, so naturally this is where we go. We are not disappointed. It is a toe-tapping fiddle extravaganza that totally blows us away. Such virtuosity! We are thrilled by Maggie Adamson who is one of Shetland's (if not Scotland's) leading fiddle players and whose dazzling brilliance gets standing ovations wherever she goes. Eunice Henderson and friends show real panache in a spirited performance, followed by the Cullivoe Fiddlers who demonstrate the unique style that has made them famous. With the Cullivoe Band to accompany the dance that follows, the night's success is assured, and to coin a phrase – a good time is had by all.

Off to Lerwick once more and with our visitors' time drawing to a close we decide to cram in a packaged tour of the sights. The museum is a must, for starters. There is so much to discover in this mini treasure house where interactive displays have been artfully designed to appeal to all ages. Two hours later we emerge very much the wiser having stepped back some 6000 years as though in a time capsule which then hurtled us through the intervening years to the present day. Every Shetlander and every tourist ought to visit the museum. It is first class. And so to the Street, the lodberries, the fort, the harbour, Clickimin Broch, Town Hall, Knab… we do it all. Commercial Street or simply 'de street' is a narrow part-pedestrianised precinct that winds seductively through the old town within gull-cry of the harbour. With its Market Cross and innumerable eateries, it is a meet-n-greet rendezvous for out of town shoppers. To either side steep and narrow flagstone lanes or 'closses' go down to the sea or up through the town, many via multiple stone stairways. It is easy to see how this ancient town gained its 'Venice of the North' label. South beyond the Small Boat Harbour towards the rocky headland known as The Knab, are the lodberries. These 18th century

warehouses and dwellings were built with their foundations in the sea making it possible for boats to moor alongside at high tide and offload merchandise by way of gantries, directly into the buildings. At one time underground passages interconnected the lodberries with houses on the hill overlooking the harbour and these passages occasionally served as conduits to bypass the watchful eye of excisemen in days when smuggling was rife – or is that just a story?

SEA VIEW

The lodberries below Lerwick's narrow streets.

Holiday over, our visitors set off on the first leg of their return journey to the antipodes where spring will greet them with its warm embrace. Meanwhile we turn our attention to the 'show' season when, in our various communities, we invite the critical eye of judges as individually we hope to win a prize for best produce, art or livestock, according to our interest. Competition is fierce even if we never quite admit it and pretend we are merely supporting the event. In a place where everyone is known to one another it is no small matter to have one's name appear on a first prize ticket and subsequently have it printed in the results page of *The Shetland Times*. With our local show in the offing we will have to see what we can do.

Midges! Holy powers! They are like to carry me off. I manage to tolerate them during the day while doing a long overdue outside painting job but come evening I make the mistake of going fishing. The loch is black calm – too calm really and you could cut the humidity with a knife. Grass and flag irises have grown to waist height since I was last here. It is to be hoped the trout have grown correspondingly. Keeping well back from the bank, I begin casting a diminutive moth-like fly. On the mirror surface it is difficult to affect a gentle touchdown and more often than not the fly looks like a jumbo jet making a crash landing in the sea. Nevertheless, it is not long before a trout is on the line – an apology for a trout actually, but at least it is over the minimum size and beggars can't be choosers. I'd like to try my luck a little longer but the midges are eating me alive. And just when I was starting to enjoy myself.

Four months into my project to create a Shetland garden, I am learning the frustrations and limitations of what lies before me. Spring most definitely did not 'burst out all over' and summer has so far been reluctant to turn up the heat. This has led to slower than expected growth and the bloomin' flowers ain't bloomin'. Perennials, which I had hoped would establish themselves sufficiently to withstand the coming winter, are much too small to survive and the hedging plants intended to provide a buffer against gales are unlikely to withstand anything stronger than a gentle breeze. But I must not be despondent. A neighbour who has lived here for several years in retirement tells me he was a career gardener in England for 40 years and none of what he learnt *there* has been of any use in establishing a garden *here*. The main difficulty lies in having to create adequate windbreaks in order to bring on tender plants. Once this is achieved it is apparent that most plants will grow despite the short season. Greenhouses, cold frames and poly-tunnels will all speed the process and most successful Shetland gardeners rely on some combination of these aids. At the end of my first summer and with little to show for it, I can see I am going to have a battle on my hands. Next year I aim to have some wind barriers in place and maybe a hothouse. Even a lukewarm house would be a step in the right direction. At least my tattie crop is far from tatty and I might even manage to pick a few peas, if you please.

One of the most telling differences between city life and that of a small island such as this is the way in which life's major milestones are celebrated by everyone This is particularly so in the case of a death. Since arriving here almost a year ago there have been several funerals and, in every instance, they have impacted on the community to a remarkable degree. Almost all the deaths have been of octogenarians or nonagenarians – highly respected people who lived exemplary lives most notable for their adherence to Christian principles. On each occasion,

SEA VIEW

the community has turned out en masse to pay their last respects, eulogising the very attributes that have been largely ignored by subsequent generations. The church is invariably packed. Words and tunes of the old hymns are obviously well-known and sung with reverence (*In the sweet by and by, we shall meet on that beautiful shore*) although the majority of the singers will not be seen in the sanctuary until the next funeral. Does that mean they might also be denied *that beautiful shore*? I hope not.

Yet surely there is an irony in the way in which a largely un-churched younger generation do this, readily acknowledging the faith of these fine old people yet unprepared to embrace it for themselves. Observing the last rites of an otherwise ignored religion seems in many ways to be a greater paradox than rejecting it outright. Or, is it simply that respect for our elders' takes precedence over faith in God?

In calm, humid weather many crofters are resorting to silage in favour of hay and not simply because they believe it to be more nutritious (a matter of some dispute when pitting the older generation against the younger). The advantage of silage is that it is a one-off cut-and-wrap process that locks in the good, while hay relies on fine weather and fresh wind for curing. If hay gets rained upon to any extent it rapidly deteriorates in quality. Not being concerned with having to feed stock in winter, I tend to view the matter from a totally different perspective. Those black poly-bags do absolutely nothing for the pastoral scene and I cannot imagine a latter-day Constable being inspired to paint the picture they present. Give me windrows of sweet hay and those beehive cones dotting the field any day.

As if to prove a point, torrential rain overnight has caused every burn and ditch to burst its banks. Crops are flattened and fences washed away. Hay is ruined. At the foaming mouth of every river, peat stained water spreads like blight across the sea's surface. There will be no hiking in the hills for a day or two as the entire landscape is a sodden sponge. There could be a plus however: the trout fishing should be good. Only one way to find out…

In light, misty rain I set out for my favourite spot. Where burn and loch converge, the surrounding marshland has become inundated and a lacy apron of froth is spreading outwards across the open water, making for ideal conditions in that I can approach the bank in my Wellington boots and cast a fly without being seen by the normally shy fish. And it works! Within a few minutes I am playing a reasonable sized trout. (Is half a pound reasonable? It is to me.) This is more like it. A second, slightly bigger one, plus two tiddlers that go back, and half an hour later I am ready to call myself a fisherman – maybe not *The Compleat Angler* but it's a start. Sweet, fresh, pan-fried trout for tea.

As if to summarise the week's weather we get a packaged version of it all in the one day – smiling dawn that is calm and clear, a mid-morning flurry of cloud that just *might* turn to rain but has second thoughts and clears off in time for a picnic lunch in hot sun. By 3pm it has changed its mind again. Sky descends to obliterate everything, temperature drops to single digits and then the wind picks up (the weatherman said it would) and by nightfall we are headed for a gale… I was about to write "never a dull moment" but that's not correct either. Weather! Who needs it?

I am beginning to think that all television stations have become obsessed with bringing us cooking programmes and weather forecasts. There is not a lot to choose between them. Both seem to rely on the presenter's ability to wave his or her hands in the manner of a conjuror about to pluck a rabbit out of a hat and to speak a load of meaningless drivel. (In the case of weather forecasters, make that drizzle.) And you can take both with a large pinch of salt. Whether it is throwing a handful of currants into a mixing bowl or ushering a shower of rain into the Home Counties, what matters is the *way* in which it is done, rather than whether the former will make a blind bit of difference to the cake or the latter is ever likely to materialise. At the end of the day we will all go to the supermarket and buy a pizza for supper, and tomorrow we will head to work with an umbrella and a sunhat to hedge our bets, because no one actually cooks any of those improbable recipes (including the TV chef who relies solely on digital enhancement), and the weather is *never* the same as the forecast. Bring back *The Magic Roundabout*, that's what I say.

Meanwhile, we have a good-going south-easterly gale to contend with. Squalls of rain are driving through the sound and The Poil is being assaulted by crashing waves. In the words of a song: "it looks like the summer is over".

By the following morning it is the storm that is over (it remains to be seen whether summer will redeem itself) and Mid Yell Regatta is able to get off to a late start, though with fewer boats on the voe than you can count on one hand it is a tame affair. Is competition sailing becoming a thing of the past? There are more spectators in the local hall where a photo exhibition of the whaling era is on show. Admittedly, most of those in attendance are old men come to relive their youth. There is a competition to guess the weight of a harpoon head. It is so heavy I can scarcely lift it off the table. One never thinks about such things when viewing old movie footage of whale hunting and it is mind boggling to imagine the effect of being struck by something like this. A photo of the graveyard at Leith in South Georgia bears witness to how dangerous the whaling industry was – and not just to whales. It is obvious many men died in that uncompromising and daunting environment. Today, so it seems, their grandchildren would sooner go to the pub and watch a footy match on TV than go sailing. Those old merchant seamen and whalers must wonder what the world is coming to.

And now we are entering upon a time of year that I have long looked forward to, when the sun moves back towards its winter quarters and begins rising south of due east. In this region I am assured of some spectacular sunrises – as was the case this morning. Eventually, in the heart of winter and from where I sit, the sun will rise out of the sea beyond the most southerly point of Fetlar. More to the point, I will be awake to see it!

Leaving Lerwick harbour on the 'sooth' boat is always an emotional experience, especially when you do not know when or if you are coming back.

SEA VIEW

Even now, when I am booked to return by the same boat tomorrow night, I am watching the old town slip by as if this is a last farewell. Mostly I am reliving all those other departures. The first when I was a ten-year-old boy bound on the adventure of a lifetime; migrating across the world and impatient to be out through the harbour heads and watch the Bressay light disappear astern, and yet… I was leaving home with all its familiar comforts and securities. It was a momentous occasion. It was to be 15 years before I came back. In doing so, I quickly came to realise that this was home and always would be. Subsequent comings and goings have never failed to evoke the same emotional responses, especially when it was by boat rather than by air. Leaving from Sumburgh by aeroplane is never quite the same. Like puffins on the nearby cliffs you whirr out over the sea and are gone in a flash. There is little time for second thoughts and, let's face it, turbo-jetting down the runway with seatbelt fastened has little to commend it when compared to standing at the stern of a ship with wind in your hair and the deck throbbing beneath your feet.

A day later with no emotional attachment whatsoever, the departure from Aberdeen nevertheless has a thrill of its own as we negotiate the narrow waterway where all manner of workhorse vessels in this busy port are being readied for voyages to who knows where. Perhaps it is the soft evening light and the ever so gentle way in which we ease away from the wharf that makes such departures evocative. And in the morning we slip back into Lerwick like a guilty child that has stayed out too late and hopes to sneak back to bed unnoticed. Was it all a dream?

Gannets are diving into the sea beyond The Poil where several rocks form a jagged reef at low tide. This is one of their favourite spots and they return to it again and again, like men who will go to long established fishing grounds in confident expectation of better catches. The gannets wheel about this region at all hours of the day but especially when the sea is relatively calm. At times, they skim the surface, rising in tight twisting aerobatics to dive on fish. At other times, they fly high into the air, working across invisible grids to quarter the region, plunging like kamikaze pilots whenever they sight a promising meal. Though they are almost a mile from the house there is no need of binoculars as gannets are substantially larger than gulls and their gleaming white plumage flashes brightly in the sunlight as they slant to and fro. Together with the play of light across the headland, this is a show I never tire of watching. People travel long distances and pay good money to see gannets. I have done so myself many years ago when I rounded Bass Rock off North Berwick on Scotland's east coast. Looking back on it now, I clearly recall the horror-tinged thrill when the tour-boat skipper sounded his ship's horn to deliberately frighten birds off the cliff face (so everyone could obtain better photos) causing innumerable eggs to go crashing down onto the rocks far below. In more enlightened times we can now only blush at such ignorance.

I have long promised myself a hike to Vigon, in Yell's far north-west corner, and today I finally get around to it. Starting early (8am) from Gloup I travel south

SEA VIEW

along the ridge above the voe. The forecast is for occasional showers but all is bright and beautiful. Reaching the head of this fjord-like voe in double quick time, I decide to detour further up the valley to Heatherdale. This valley is the shortest route between Gloup and the head of Basta Voe and in bygone days, when Gloup was a haaf fishing station, men from east and west Yell would travel this route to help crew the sixareens. In those days there was a shop at Heatherdale from which travellers could stock up on food for the journey – 'faerdie-maet' as it was then termed. The attraction today is not the shop, which is long gone together with the valley's population, but to find a plantation of trees and shrubs which was established in this lovely spot by members of the Cullivoe community. The project has certainly proved to be successful and is a credit to those who planned it. A small copse which incorporates a variety of conifers, together with beeches, willows, birches and rowans, is well established. Some of the trees are already over 25 feet high. It is to be hoped future generations will maintain the rabbit-proof fence or this little oasis in the 'wilds o Yell' might not survive.

Having thoroughly explored this beautiful though lonely spot where the ruins of several buildings are all that is left of a once significant way-station, I turn once more for Vigon where a certain cave and the story surrounding it has become something of a legend in my lifetime. During the war, when I was a toddler and living in Cullivoe, the local Home Guard was called out to combat what was believed to be the long-feared German invasion. What followed was a farce the like of which would have made great viewing on the TV series *Dad's Army*. The men assembled at Gloup rather too late in the day for action and so bivouacked until morning when at dawn they rowed across the voe and proceeded to march on Vigon. Each man had been issued with ten rounds of .303 ammunition of which five had already been expended on target practice. The expected battle was likely to be brief and bloody.

Crossing that open moor today, I try to imagine what it would have felt like for those few old men who, having received a report of machine-gun fire, had no reason to doubt it. They could not seriously have had any hope of halting an invasion with five rounds of ammunition each. Of course, there was no invasion. The machine-gun fire was to do with the cave I mentioned – a cave that these selfsame elderly crofters had filled with salvaged wood from the beach at Vigon and which the government 'Wood Boat' had discovered. The cave was high up in a cliff and, unfortunately, the Cullivoe men had filled it rather too full of their illegally salvaged wood. What had happened was that the crew of the Wood Boat had come ashore, placed an explosive charge under the cave's entrance and then detonated it with rifle fire from offshore, causing the wood to cascade back down the cliff face to the beach from where the officially appointed salvagers removed it to their boat. My father told the story in his memoirs (*The Upstander*, The Shetland Times Ltd., 1977) and I have forever wanted to find where this comedy of errors took place. Why? I can't rightly say. Perhaps it is that growing up with the story I have always felt admiration for those brave men who set out to protect their village in the only way they could and, doubtless, knowing full well that it was a forlorn hope. I have wondered too at who their real enemies were – the Germans or the bumptious resource-wasting officials who denied them their little bit of hard-won salvage.

Returning across the moor I reach a high point from which I can see all the way back to Mid Yell – in other words half the island – and I now realise that the remote ruins at Lumbister which I visited some months ago are not really so remote. All the settlements, like the people themselves, are interconnected and interdependent and would have been much more so a century or two ago.

As teenagers, my younger brother and I used to go fishing for flounder in the sandy tidal flats around the coast of Tasmania. We fished at night on an incoming tide, wading waist deep and towing a large inflated inner tube over which we had built a raft to hold our gear. Besides handmade spears (broomsticks with a short length of sharpened fencing wire fixed to one end) we had a 12-volt battery connected to a sealed beam car headlight. The light was held under the water to illuminate the seabed.

Flounder can be extremely difficult to see as they bury themselves in the soft sand at the slightest hint of danger; however, this action generally creates a tiny tell-tale puff of sand in the midst of which a sharp-eyed hunter can detect the two black dots (eyes) on top of the slightly domed head. With one of us holding the light, the other positioned his spear directly above and between those dots. Stabbing swiftly then sweeping the spear in a forward and upward arc, the fish was brought to the surface upside-down on the spike. A quick flick of the wrist transferred the catch to a deep basin on the raft. Any hesitation and the flounder would escape, as there was no barb on the wire spike.

It was easy to become disorientated wading in the dark with all our attention focussed on the arc of light beneath the sea and sometimes we found ourselves going too far out with the incoming tide filling deep channels between us and the shore. Not that this created a problem as we were good swimmers and could generally distinguish the tree-ed skyline against the night sky and make our way ashore.

On one occasion, we were confronted by a giant sting-ray that came languidly flapping into the circle of light. It looked big enough to eat us! In our panic, we jerked the power leads off the battery and almost upset the tyre tube. It was then a case of floundering in the dark with flounder being the last thing on our minds as we beat a hasty retreat.

With equinoctial gales back on the agenda, I hear tell of 148kph wind gusts and 18 metre waves off the southern coast of Tasmania. Roaring Forties indeed! No such drama here – yet.

While this account spans a single year only, it has almost seven decades of hindsight to back it. That is a lifetime and in it Shetland has changed dramatically. Not the environment; not the weather or the wildlife – they are essentially the same. What has changed is the people who live here and the lifestyle they lead.

SEA VIEW

These changes are less evident in the main town of Lerwick where many still live in the same houses in which their grandparents did – albeit with mod cons. It is in the small declining crofting communities where differences are most notable. Where in my youth everyone grew rigs of corn, neeps and tatties; cut their own fuel from the peat bank; milked a cow and kept hens and sheep; now the rigs are in the sea – oil rigs, mussel racks and salmon cages. The majority of the folk have de-crofted their land to leave it lying fallow and have built modern all-electric bungalows to live in. They have pursued a wage outside of their village, in most cases working for local government or multi-national companies. The village halls, once the focal point of all communal activity, have been lavishly modernised though whether they are utilised to the same extent is a moot point. Television and all forms of information technology reign supreme at the expense of the WRI, the kirk and other out-moded forms of social intercourse. Everyone is better off financially, flying away to Portugal, Turkey or the Seychelles for holidays. A day trip to Lerwick was an 'experience' fifty years ago and a weekend in Aberdeen was beyond the means of most. Now there are drugs on the street where once there were drunks, wheelchair access to all public buildings to facilitate entry for an aging population and smoke alarms to hurry them out again should any be foolish enough to light a fag or get hot under the collar. Leisure centres are all the rage despite everyone apparently having no time to use them or become too obese to leave their armchairs. And, if any *should* dare to venture out, Big Brother is waiting behind CCTV cameras to make sure they mind their Ps and Qs. We used to speak of the "good old days" but that is now infra-dig. They were actually "bad old days" and you better believe it because "we have never had it so good". How do I know? Because we have replaced our witch-doctors with spin-doctors and they tell us it is so. Oh yes, things have changed!

A trawl through this account of a year in Shetland will reveal that, contrary to what most people seem to believe, the isles are not constantly being battered by huge seas and gale force winds; quite the opposite in fact. By far the majority of days have been relatively calm and today is yet another of the same. Two small fishing boats are sitting proud in the middle of the sound. A child's toys discarded on a polished table. In a fit of pique I might reach out a hand and sweep them away, except to do so would in all probability deny me the chance of a fish supper… and surprise, surprise, a fish supper comes my way. Straight out of the sea and freshly filleted. I could grow to like this place!

And now with summer behind us what does the weather do? It turns to summer. Wouldn't you know it? Not that anyone is complaining. I have always said autumn is the best season of the year – what with its 'mellow fruitfulness' and all that harvesting of crops for the coming winter. I think it is the squirrel in me. I love making jams and pickles, bottling fruit and packing the deep freeze with home-grown vegetables. Now, let's see what the show judges make of my rhubarb jam and marmalade…

Yell show day turns out to be a great success and a credit to the island's scattered little villages that work so harmoniously each year to bring it about.

SEA VIEW

There is nothing like a show for bringing out the best in people: their best exhibits and their best efforts. The East Yell community hall and its surrounds is a buzzing hive of activity all day. Perfect weather. Big crowd. No strangers – only friends and family – that is what makes Shetland special. Loads of hard work and lots of fun. Sheep, cattle, ponies, pets, home-bakes, crafts, flowers, garden produce, and more. Every pen is full of prize-worthy animals; every table groans under the weight of excellence it displays. There is all the usual sideshow razzmatazz and the band plays on… and on. Adaline wins a rosette for 'Reserve Overall Item in the Show' and comes home with a stack of other prizes (modesty precludes me from mentioning my own minor successes). But it is not about winning, it is about community spirit. A chance to show off a little and to share in celebrating another successful harvest; congratulate one another on our endeavours and strive to keep up the standards that ensure our livestock and crops will continue to thrive. Winter can be long and cold in these parts. We need these special days to look back upon.

In this spell of fine weather I am able to watch the sanguine sunrise each morning as it comes flooding in my bedroom window to wake me. It is only a couple of weeks since I began taking particular note of the compass bearing and already it has moved several points further to the south where soon it will no longer be behind Fetlar but will rise directly out of the sea. At this latitude the path of the sun from summer to winter solstice is nothing short of amazing. Earlier in the year I asked an old man who had lived in the one spot all his life if he could tell me where the sun set on midsummer's eve from his particular perspective. He said he wasn't rightly sure. I found this hard to believe. Have we become so indifferent to nature and our environment that we no longer notice the very sun? What would our ancestors think of such blatant disregard of their god?

Tomorrow I will come full circle having begun this on 12th September, 2009. It is time to begin drawing these threads together and to collect my final thoughts now that the year has all but run its course. Back then I was full of trepidation of what the future held, having left family and friends in Australia and come – some might say on a whim – to find my roots. Was I doing the right thing? A year is hardly long enough in which to find the answer to that question but so far it *feels* right. In all of my life, no matter where I have travelled, Shetland has always meant 'home'. As if to reassure me, today's sea is at its sparkling best and I am lured out once more to try and record it on film…

SEA VIEW

In addition to this photograph, taken on the beach below my house, I also took the one chosen for the front cover. These two pictures are, for me, the very essence of Shetland. The sea breaking on a rocky beach and, somewhere nearby, a boat. A true Shetlander ought to ask for nothing more.

And now, on this last day, I am wondering how best to summarise my year of reflective glimpses into life by the sea in Shetland. There can be no definitive statement. I have tried photography at all times of the day and night and never managed to capture it to my entire satisfaction. I have watched the play of light and shade over The Poil as wind harries clouds across the sky and I cannot find words to adequately express it. The ever-changing moods of the sea go far and beyond my puny attempts to describe them.

Over six months ago I wrote: "All who come here inevitably become enchanted and however much circumstances might dictate the need to return to another place you will forever be compelled to come back again and again". This is the magic of these islands. It is inescapable. So come, if you dare, and be prepared to be entranced. You may never be the same again and, like me, you may not want to leave…

GLOSSARY

Shetland words unless otherwise stated

affrug the back-surge of waves after having broken on the shore
ayre a beach or sandy headland
baa a sunken or partially submerged rock
bach (New Zealand) holiday house, shack
bairn child
banksflooers thrift
banks rekk timber of any sort that has been washed up by the sea
bannock scone
bat a light puff of wind
böl a shelter or wind-break for animals
bonhoga childhood home
brennastyooch fine spray rising from sea breaking on a shore
bretsh the breaking of waves on a shore
broch Iron Age circular stone tower
bruck rubbish
De Aald Rock sentimental name for Shetland
ert direction
faerdy-maet food for a journey
firth wide sea inlet
flan downdraft of wind or sudden squall
flukra large flakes (of snow)
fram out to sea
geo a cleft in a rock, esp. on a rocky coast; a ravine into which sea-water flows
gooster strong gust of wind
gremster an exceptionally low ebb-tide
guff puff of wind
haaf deep-sea fishing
hamefir home-coming celebration
hap shawl
holm small island
löragub sea-spume, especially thick foam piled in a narrow space by heavy sea
meids prominent features on land by which fishermen take bearings

105

SEA VIEW

merry dancers aurora
moder-dy mother wave – an underlying swell that always sets landward
irrespective of wind direction and by which experienced seamen once took
their bearings
moorit brown
ness a headland or promontory
nipsiccar bitter
noost a natural hollow or scooped out trench (sometimes walled) at the
beachhead, into which a boat is drawn up and secured; a boat-shed
pau shell (New Zealand) abalone shell
peerie small
piltock coalfish (two to four years old)
platt maalie calm flat calm
roost a strong tidal current
saatbrack the spray and foam from breaking waves.
shoormal high tide mark; the turning point of waves breaking on a beach
shorebod breaking sea
sixareen six-oared open boat used at the haaf fishing
skudd lumps of foam on the surface of the sea; a drifting mass being driven in
to the shore by waves
snaar the turn of the tide; a tide rip
sungaets clockwise; the path of the sun
tievin thieving
Thule Shetland
trow supernatural being from Scandinavian mythology (troll) passed into
Shetland folklore
trow hadd trow den or dwelling
tushkar Shetland peat-cutting tool
voe a narrow sea inlet
weel kent well known
yowe ewe

Note: All Shetland place-names are according to Ordnance Survey maps nos.
466, 467, 468, 469 and 470; scale 1:25,000

All photos are of 7 mega pixel definition and taken by the author (unless
otherwise stated) using a Panasonic digital camera Model DMC-FZ8 and having
a 12X optical zoom.

About the Author

ALASTAIR Christie-Johnston was born in Cullivoe, North Yell, and began his education at Happyhansel School, Walls. He spent most of his adult life in Tasmania, Australia, where he wrote *Nor Heard the Clock Strike* (The Shetland Times Ltd., 2004) and *Mountain View* (Wellington Park Management Trust, 2008). He returned to live in Shetland in 2009 where he and his wife completed *Shetland Words - A dictionary of the Shetland dialect* which was published by The Shetland Times Ltd. in 2010. His latest work *The Ninian Plate*, a Shetland novel, is due for release later this year (2011) also by The Shetland Times Ltd. He also is a regular contributor to the local monthly magazine *Shetland Life*.